ID0983054

The publisher gratefully acknowledges the generous support of the Atkinson Family Imprint in Higher Education of the University of California Press Foundation, which was established by a major gift from the Atkinson Family Foundation.

Searching for Utopia

THE CLARK KERR LECTURES ON
THE ROLE OF HIGHER EDUCATION
IN SOCIETY

1. *The American Research University from World War II to World Wide Web: Governments, the Private Sector, and the Emerging Meta-University,* by Charles M. Vest

2. *Searching for Utopia: Universities and Their Histories,* by Hanna Holborn Gray

3. *Higher Education: The Play of Continuity and Crisis,* by Neil J. Smelser

Searching for Utopia

Universities and Their Histories

Hanna Holborn Gray

UNIVERSITY OF CALIFORNIA PRESS

Berkeley   Los Angeles   London

CENTER FOR STUDIES IN HIGHER EDUCATION

Berkeley

The Center for Studies in Higher Education at the University of California, Berkeley, is a multidisciplinary research and policy center on higher education oriented to California, the nation, and comparative international issues. CSHE promotes discussion among university leaders, government officials, and academics; assists policy making by providing a neutral forum for airing contentious issues; and keeps the higher education world informed of new initiatives and proposals. The Center's research aims to inform current debate about higher education policy and practice.

University of California Press, one of the most distinguished university presses in the United States, enriches lives around the world by advancing scholarship in the humanities, social sciences, and natural sciences. Its activities are supported by the UC Press Foundation and by philanthropic contributions from individuals and institutions. For more information, visit www.ucpress.edu.

University of California Press
Berkeley and Los Angeles, California

University of California Press, Ltd.
London, England

Library of Congress Cataloging-in-Publication Data

Gray, Hanna Holborn.
Searching for Utopia : universities and their histories / Hanna Holborn Gray.
    p.   cm.—(Clark Kerr lectures on the role of higher education in society ; 2)
Includes bibliographical references.
ISBN 978-0-520-27065-7 (cloth : alk. paper)
ISBN 978-0-520-95170-9 (ebook)
    1. Education, Higher—Aims and objectives—United States.   I. Title.
LA227.4.G737 2012
378.73—dc23

                                                                                    2011036637

Manufactured in the United States of America

21 20 19 18 17 16 15 14 13 12
10 9 8 7 6 5 4 3 2 1

In keeping with a commitment to support environmentally responsible and sustainable printing practices, UC Press has printed this book on Rolland Enviro100, a 100% post-consumer fiber paper that is FSC certified, deinked, processed chlorine-free, and manufactured with renewable biogas energy. It is acid-free and EcoLogo certified.

CONTENTS

Preface vii

Introduction
1

1. *The Uses of the University* Revisited
7

2. The University Idea and Liberal Learning
31

3. Uses (and Misuses) of the University Today
61

Conclusion
93

Notes 97

Select Bibliography 113

PREFACE

The lectures assembled in this volume were presented as the Clark Kerr Lectures on Higher Education at the University of California in fall 2009. I am grateful to all who made my visit to Berkeley so interesting and rewarding, and above all to Judson King, director of the Center for Studies in Higher Education. I should like also to acknowledge my indebtedness to William G. Bowen, Mary Patterson McPherson, and Judith Shapiro for their helpful comments; to Charles M. Gray for innumerable and always enlightening discussions; and to the readers for the University of California Press for their suggestions.

At several points, I have drawn closely on some of my earlier essays. In chapter 2, the discussion of Eliot, Harper, and Wilson follows in part from "The Leaning Tower of Academe," *Bulletin of the American Academy of Arts and Sciences* 49 (1996): 34–54; and that of the desirability of requiring courses in Western civilization from "Western Civilization and Its Discontents," *Historically*

Speaking 7 (2005): 41–42. Chapter 3 also repeats some conclusions of "The Leaning Tower of Academe."

Finally, more books and articles on the subject of higher education (and its failings, real and alleged) appear almost every day. A great many have been published since the time when these lectures were written. Still more will appear before they are printed. I have included in the notes and bibliography just a few of the more recent publications, either because (like Hacker and Arum) they are the subjects of considerable attention or because (like Archibald and Feldman) they seem of particular value in illuminating their subjects.

Introduction

The essays that follow are not intended to offer anything approaching a comprehensive view of the state of higher education today but to reflect on some perennial questions and debates that have accompanied the history of American research universities and that continue to be addressed today. They were presented as the Clark Kerr Lectures on Higher Education at the Berkeley and Davis campuses of the University of California in fall 2009. I had known and admired Clark Kerr as perhaps the most thoughtful and incisive commentator on American higher education in the late twentieth century, and rereading his *The Uses of the University*, first published in 1963, confirmed that earlier judgment. So in these lectures named for him, I undertook to consider to what extent his analysis of the research university, as he then described it, might still be descriptive of that institution and its essential features in our time.

I was struck by the sense in which Kerr's depiction offered a decidedly mixed review of the character, achievement, and prospects of the postwar university. In coining the term, and in laying out the nature, of the "multiversity," Kerr was not so much defending as trying dispassionately to picture the anatomy of the research university as it had come to dominance in the academic universe, to explain the confluence of causes that had created its character and strengths, and to assess the losses and potential weaknesses as well as the gains represented in its current state.

I was struck also by Kerr's several references to another major figure of twentieth-century higher education, Robert Maynard Hutchins of the University of Chicago. It seemed clear that the two were far apart in their views and in their experience, but Kerr spoke of himself and Hutchins as the principal critics and reformers of their time. To compare them is to contrast two ways of thinking about universities that can be roughly identified with the ideas of the "collegiate university" and the "multiversity." They remain still the two broad and opposing models that one finds cited in contemporary discussions of the university.[1] One may in addition differentiate the two styles of an uncompromising idealist, in the case of Hutchins, and a pragmatic realist, in that of Kerr. Yet if Hutchins appears the ultimate utopian, Kerr saw himself also as pursuing a utopian goal—but as doing so with the knowledge that there were no guarantees ever of perfection in "the eternal search for utopia"[2] and with the conviction that the fate of this mandated search was only partially in the power of the universities themselves to determine.

The contrast between Hutchins and Kerr, then, seemed to reveal the two most familiar forms in which the American research university has been conceived. At the same time, their discussions of higher education display some equally visible commonalities, not only in their "searching for utopia," but also in many of the concerns to which their critiques were directed.

Increasingly, it appeared, from a historical perspective, that the issues to which they pointed had already been those animating the essential questions associated with liberal learning from centuries long past together with others that spoke to the key controversies over the purposes and conditions of universities from the time of their emergence in late-nineteenth-century America. Hence it seemed worthwhile to ask how the collegiate idea of a university founded in a tradition of the liberal arts came into being, how it was affected by new intellectual movements and assumptions (including a redefinition of the content of liberal learning itself), how it was seen to be challenged by a new commitment to research and scholarship and graduate training and by the growth of professionalism and specialization that marked the development of the universities, even while claiming to reconcile these sometimes conflicting directions in an integral idea of a single university culture.

The third theme of these essays has to do with the history of major debates, responsive to the conditions of the multiversity described by Kerr and to subsequent events and developments, in the decades since he wrote, and finally with some assessment of the questions surrounding the situation of the research university today. To a large degree, Kerr's anxieties about the signs of trouble he detected in the multiversity of his day—the lessening sense and reality of a focused academic community with the continuing march of specialization casting up further internal barriers; the dynamic of continuing institutional growth, diversification, and intellectual fragmentation; the proliferation of activities and programs within the university and of demands

on it from without; the conflicted loyalties of faculties; the problem of maintaining attention to undergraduate instruction in
research-dominated environments; the declining emphasis on
liberal learning and the humanities—remain still the anxieties, often indeed intensified, of our present. At the same time,
the context in which these make their appearance has altered,
shaped by developments that Kerr could hardly have foreseen in
1963, the technological revolution above all, but also, for example,
the broadening, with its accompanying controversies, of access
for women and minorities.

As to the present, my commentary touches rather rapidly on
a variety of issues that seem to me of special weight and impact.
It was intended to stimulate the more extended discussions that
lectures can provoke. As it happened, these lectures took place
at just the time when the severe financial problems confronting
the University of California, and the battles surrounding them,
had reached a kind of climax. Demonstrations, sit-ins, and brief
occupations of buildings were taking place. The immediate spark
had to do with a recommendation before the Regents to increase
tuition by some 30 percent, approved against the background
of extensive budget cuts, layoffs, and mandatory furloughs that
had already provoked strong reaction. The longer-term questions under debate had to do with the University of California
itself, its role and mission, its quality and future. But these had to
do also with the outlook for public higher education more
generally (including the very large questions of its social
responsibilities, of the perceived shifts, and their import, toward
"privatization" for the flagship universities in particular, and of
whether contemporary events would have a disproportionate
effect on the public universities) and with the prospects for all

of higher education in a time of recession and of looking to an increasingly uncertain period ahead.

Once again, as at successive moments in the previous decades, the theme of the day was that of crisis in the world of higher education, and this crisis seemed magnified beyond the difficulties of earlier times. Its elements were connected not only to economic disaster, but to the perception of a sharp decline in public support, understanding, and respect for the purposes of universities and a mounting tide of criticism of their performance.

In the end, the difficulties faced by the research universities today cannot be dismissed as though they were simply signs of yet another episode in a long line of asserted crises. On the contrary, it seems to me that our difficulties would need to be addressed even in the absence of the economic circumstances that have dramatized their scope. We cannot assume that a time of contraction will inevitably be succeeded by one of prosperity in which our institutions can return to what had been the assumptions of business as usual. In arguing for a turn to what I call the "stripped down" university—that is, a university leaner, more selective in aspiration and more focused in purpose, I am not imagining a return to some golden model of the past or some single model of an ideal institution or some simple means of transforming the highly complex institutional patterns of the present. My hope would be rather for a redirection aimed at strengthening the differentiations and collaborations within the world of universities and at acknowledging and reanimating the basic principles and priorities of education, learning, and discovery that define their best possibilities.

ONE

The Uses of the University
Revisited

Clark Kerr's *The Uses of the University*, first published in 1963, is still, I think, the best book on American higher education written in the twentieth century. It is a marvel of terseness and clarity that lays bare the complexities and subtleties of a complicated topic. It details with precision and wit the anatomy of the research university as it had come to exist in 1963, and it describes as well the illnesses to which this organism could be prone together with diagnoses and prognoses that might prove useful. And, of course, it indelibly impressed the word *multiversity* as the descriptor of the postwar research university.

That a work so lucid should have provoked so much misunderstanding and misreading is quite remarkable, even allowing for the temper of the time of gathering dissidence in which it appeared. Critics of the research university (and most immediately, critics at the University of California) interpreted the book as a single-minded defense of the multiversity and of the established social and political order with which it was complicit and heard its analytic tone as the impersonal and bureaucratic voice of a corporate institution that had turned away from the humane values that ought to define a genuine community of learning.

Clark Kerr was a man both rational and reasonable to the nth degree, and he found it difficult to cope with reactions to his work that seemed to be neither. For all his patience and good sense and Quakerly tolerance, he resented such misinterpretation and refused to let it go. He thought it obvious that he was actually offering a quite critical analysis of some very troubling attributes and tendencies of the contemporary university and making the point that the contemporary research university represented an institution of extraordinary promise and accomplishment that was here to stay and whose history could not be undone but that its growth had also exacted significant costs and might, left to the logic of its own dynamic development, exact yet further and possibly fatal ones. Kerr responded to his critics by trying, over and over again and ultimately in his memoirs, to state and to restate what he had really meant. And he regularly wrote to bring his analysis up to date, as he did in the successive chapters written for later editions of *The Uses of the University*, and elsewhere as well, at different moments conveying varying degrees of cautious optimism or moderate pessimism in taking the temperature of the patient he had followed throughout his career.

Beneath the wise, sensible, calm, unpretentious, and visibly stoical person of Clark Kerr, there appeared in his dogged quest for a kind of vindication a man more driven, one who, after the experience and circumstances of his tenure as chancellor and president, felt that he had still more to teach, that he had gained and refined an essential knowledge through which he could leave a larger impact on the academic world than had perhaps been acknowledged. But being Clark Kerr, a principled man of strong ideals, and an intelligent realist above all, he was also wryly aware of claiming that belief and never lost his capacity for disinterested commentary and generous judgment.

So it is something of a surprise to find Kerr, in his 1994 addendum to *The Uses of the University*, looking back to 1963 and asking:

> Would I have chosen to give these lectures when I did knowing what I know now? The answer is absolutely "no."
>
> The next question is whether I should have given these lectures as an active president regardless of the date, and the answer is "almost certainly not." Only one other sitting president in the twentieth century, to my knowledge, was as openly critical of the modern research university as I was, and that was Robert Maynard Hutchins. We shared some (but by no means all) of the same reasons, and he paid for his criticism. He was the more critical . . . and the more acerbic and eloquent in his comments. He attempted to do far more about his criticisms, and he also paid the more for it. The almost universal presidential pattern is to speak in laudatory platitudes, and never to be indiscreet—better to be "pompous." This is not only what is routinely offered but also what is confidently expected and placidly accepted. I have concluded that it is a disservice to the presidency to speak otherwise; that it is not wise to be as frank and open as Bob Hutchins and I were; that discretion is the better part of valor—a rule that most presidents do not have to be told to obey.[1]

I don't know that these words reflect Kerr's final thoughts on the subject, but they are interesting nonetheless in the familiar questions they raise about the nature of a university president's responsibility in matters of public utterance, and interesting also in their assessment of Robert Maynard Hutchins.

In some ways, I would expect Hutchins to be the last person to whom Kerr might compare himself. Hutchins set out deliberately to play the role of enfant terrible and revolutionary; indeed, he was to say that a president's function is precisely to be a troublemaker.[2] He believed that only one model of higher education could be of value, and he saw its mission as leading ultimately to the spiritual transformation of a corrupt and materialistic world that had lost all sense of purpose and descended into a dark well of skeptical relativism, scientism, empty empiricism, false vocationalism, and anti-intellectualism. His comment that the University of Chicago was not a very good university but only the best there was spoke to his pained sense of the chasm separating the world of academe from the ideal he believed it should embody. Hutchins was impatient with compromise and incremental change, and he was deeply frustrated by what he saw as the inertia and resistance to change prevalent in universities. Those qualities he attributed to the debilitating weaknesses of academic governance and to the triumph of professionalism and specialization in the academy.

To call Hutchins "outspoken" is something of an understatement. Let us consider for a few moments his critique of contemporary higher education, his conception of the university and its appropriate structure, and the program of education he advocated.

Hutchins maintained that the modern university lacked all unity of intellectual purpose and failed to offer an education in the fundamental ideas and questions that should shape human thought and investigation. He deplored the excessive specialization that he saw as overwhelming the world of learning and as reinforced by the departmental system; the obstructions this system placed in the way of a common, broader, and deeper intellectual association among the university's members; and what he regarded as a practice and culture of undergraduate education diametrically opposed to the liberal learning, founded in a curriculum of general education, that he sought to establish at Chicago and that he believed could stand as a universal model for higher education. In striking out against what he described as the intellectual disorder and triviality that had overtaken the university, Hutchins was also railing against something more— namely, against the evils that he believed had overtaken the modern world and that threatened civilization itself.

His first big public salvos against modern higher education were delivered in a series of lectures published as *The Higher Learning in America* (a title and in some respects an argument that echoed Thorstein Veblen's strident critique of some twenty years before). We live, he said, in a philistine world in which even universities are fundamentally anti-intellectual and in which universities hence suffer internal disunity and intellectual anarchy rather than display the singleness of purpose and clarity on the subject of the central questions of truth that should mark the true university.

> The college, we say, is for social adaptation; the university is for vocational. Nowhere does insistence on intellectual problems as the only problems worthy of a university's consideration meet with such opposition as in the universities themselves.[3]

> Why is it that the chief characteristic of the higher learning is disorder? It is because there is no ordering principle in it. . . . *The common aim of all parts of a university may and should be the pursuit of the truth for its own sake.* But this common aim is not sufficiently precise to hold the university together while it is moving toward it. Real

unity can be achieved only by a hierarchy of truths which shows us which are fundamental and which subsidiary, which significant and which not.[4]

He went on to cite the medieval university as based on a foundation of unity emanating from theology and a rational order of study proceeding from first principles. For theology, said Hutchins, it was now necessary to substitute metaphysics. "Without theology or metaphysics," he asserted, "a unified university cannot exist,"[5] and he proceeded to claim that "[i]f we can revitalize metaphysics and restore it to its place in the higher learning, we may be able to establish rational order in the modern world as well as in the universities."[6]

Hutchins believed, as he put it later:

> The last half century has substituted confusion and bewilderment for the simple faith in the light of which the universities carried on their work. The civilization which we thought so well established seems on the verge of dissolution. The religious belief which led so many denominations to found universities does not sustain their constituencies today. Instead of feeling that we were born with a common inheritance of ideas about the purposes of the state and the destiny of man, we listen to competing affirmations of contradictory positions on these issues without being able either to accept or deny them in a manner satisfactory to ourselves.[7]

> The centrifugal forces released through the dissolution of ultimate beliefs have split the universities into a thousand fragments. When men begin to doubt whether there is such a thing as truth or whether it can ever be discovered, the search for truth must lose that precision which it had in the minds of those who founded the American universities. . . . The universities, instead of leading us through the chaos of the modern world, mirror its confusion.[8]

It is here that the central convictions animating Hutchins's critique of higher education and his advocacy for general education come together with his despair over the state of the world. If the world were to be saved, it would be through education, but education had first to be transformed. To reestablish what he called a rational order in the world meant to restore a rational, and hierarchical, order to the world of knowledge and of thought. It meant eliminating the perverse effects of free elective systems, of a random and superficial education summed up by courses and credits and pursued in the interest of social skills and vocational outcomes, by creating instead a program of general education. It meant the recognition that there existed a distinctive content of "permanent studies" that every educated person had to have mastered and an acceptance of what Hutchins presented as irrefutable logic: "Education implies teaching. Teaching implies knowledge. Knowledge is truth. The truth is everywhere the same. Hence education should be everywhere the same."[9]

You will have noticed that Hutchins refers in his commentary to better times. One is the world of the medieval university, another the golden age of ancient Greece; a third, somewhat oddly, is the time of the founding of the American universities, including that of the University of Chicago whose founder actually wanted to establish a research institution above all and even wondered seriously whether it should have an undergraduate college that included the first two years. (And who, it should be added, initiated the formidable era of Amos Alonzo Stagg football at the university.) Finally, you will have observed that Hutchins's strictures on what he saw as the hopeless state of the university rest on his fundamental disagreement with what he regarded as the triumph of "scientism," "empiricism," and "presentism" in disciplinary research and scholarship, relativism in the realm of thought, and utilitarian considerations of the most philistine sort in the field of education, both undergraduate and professional.

For Hutchins the elective system championed by Charles William Eliot was the emblem of higher education's fall from the grace of a required liberal curriculum incorporating a hierarchy of truth.

> Here the great criminal was Mr. Eliot, who as President of Harvard applied his genius, skill and longevity to the task of robbing American youth of their cultural heritage. Since he held that there were no such things as good or bad subjects of study, his laudable effort to open the curriculum to good ones naturally led him to open it to bad ones and finally to destroy it altogether. . . . The crucial error is that of holding that nothing is any more important than anything else, that there can be no order of goods and no order in the intellectual realm. There is nothing central and nothing peripheral, nothing primary and nothing secondary, nothing basic and nothing superficial. The course of study goes to pieces because there is nothing to hold it together. Triviality, mediocrity, and vocationalism take it over because we have no standard by which to judge them.[10]

As president of the University of Chicago, Hutchins became increasingly frustrated by the conflicts generated by his energetic attempts to have his views and plans adopted and by the snail's pace of movement he thought had been accomplished. He had come to believe that for a university to work, its system of governance, its organization, and some of its traditional policies and practices needed to be overhauled if any progress were ever to be made in the face of the inertia and opposition that seemed to prevail everywhere under the status quo. He would have liked to abolish departments, and he would have liked to place academic areas dealing with policy and applied studies into separate research institutes affiliated with the university (their members would not have the status of regular faculty members; in this way those not dealing with what he considered truly fundamental studies would be outside the unity of the university proper). These were general preferences that he floated from time to time. And he did effect two significant organizational changes in the creation of the four graduate divisions, physical sciences, biological sciences, social sciences, and humanities, that were intended to promote interdisciplinary vistas, as well as the creation of the college as a division in itself with responsibility for a bachelor's degree awarded after the successful conclusion of Chicago's program of general education. He had famously provoked outrage in some quarters and joy in others by eliminating Big Ten football at the University of Chicago. That move underscored his notion of what a college should not be about, although he joked that had he not abolished football, the Humane Society would have had to be called in for that purpose.

In 1944, in a speech to the faculty and trustees, Hutchins finally decided to throw all discretion to the winds and to challenge his own university by proposing a comprehensive list of the concrete steps needed to reshape the institutional university, ones that he knew would really shake things up.[11] He began by saying it was necessary to abolish academic rank, adopt a compensation system that paid individuals according to their financial need, compel professors to return all outside earnings to the university, and establish a separate institute of liberal studies to award the Ph.D. as a teaching degree for a new academic profession of teaching general education. At the same time he appealed again for an end to traditional courses and credits and what he called the "adding machine system of education." He called instead for the adoption of a B.A. program that would admit high school juniors and seniors into a college of general education that would formally last two years, with degrees awarded on the basis of comprehensive examinations in the fundamental fields to be taken when a student was ready. The principal outlines of this curriculum were at last established at Chicago toward the later years of Hutchins's presidency, and his college became an educational experiment and, for a time, an educational success, of a unique kind. Nor did it ever cease to be controversial. "The University of Chicago's undergraduate college," wrote A.J. Liebling in 1952, "acts as the greatest magnet for juvenile neurotics since the Children's Crusade, with Robert Maynard Hutchins, the institution's renovator, . . . playing the role of Stephen the Shepherd Boy in the revival."[12]

Hutchins's major proposal, one that he made a condition for achieving all the rest, was to redefine the authority of the presidential office. Arguing that divided authority meant that no one could ever be truly accountable and nothing significant could ever get done, pointing to the weakness he thought inherent in any separation of powers in the universe of politics as in that of the university, Hutchins asked that he be given full authority over all academic matters. The president would be expected to consult the faculty on his initiatives, but their advice would be strictly advisory. The president would be elected for a limited term of office, and constitutional provisions would be made for the recall of a president should he lose the confidence of the faculty. The statutes of the university, in his suggested draft, would state that the president had "full responsibility for and full authority over the educational and scholarly work of the University, its course of study, publications, appointments to its faculty, and all other matters relating to its activities in education and research."[13]And yet, Hutchins maintained, his organization of the university would actually lead to a more democratic community by reducing the preponderant power of the senior faculty and extending the same rights to those previously excluded from the faculty senate.

All his recommended actions, according to Hutchins, were means to accomplish the purpose of the university, referring to this as a "crusade." That purpose, he said, "is nothing less than to procure a moral, intellectual, and spiritual revolution throughout the world. The whole scale of values by which our society lives must be reversed if any society is to endure. We want a democratic academic community because we know that if we have one we can multiply the power which the University can bring to bear upon the character, the mind, and the spirit of men."[14]

As you can well imagine, the speech I have summarized caused much consternation. Above all, the last words I have quoted were taken to suggest a desire on Hutchins's part to impose an ideological conformity threatening to the intellectual freedom at the core of the university. He was forced to try to persuade his colleagues that he had intended nothing of the kind, but the suspicions, and the sense of his overreaching claims to a new authority, initiated a period of crisis in the university that brought a heightened debate to the questions of university governance and purpose. In the end, of course, academic rank, differential compensation, a single set of Ph.D. requirements, and an affirmation of faculty participation in all essential areas of educational policy remained in effect.[15]

It should be noted that Hutchins had no qualms about publicly stating his views also on matters quite outside the subject of education and firing off rhetorical bombshells on these subjects as well. Shortly after his arrival in Chicago, he addressed a Democratic convention with a passionate argument for repudiating and overturning the failed policies of the older generation that had produced society's ruined condition. At the end of the thirties, Hutchins became a convinced isolationist, hoping to persuade the world in general and college students in particular to oppose and resist America's entry into war.[16] Hutchins was a man of charisma, especially for college students, and a man of great rhetorical skill and force. He used these gifts both within and outside the university to campaign for his beliefs without making any particular distinction between those that had to do with education and those that did not. In his way of thinking, any such distinction would in any case have been quite meaningless.

Given this history, there is nothing unusual in Clark Kerr citing Hutchins as the outspoken president of the twentieth century. Since Hutchins's day, many people, including many who have never read Hutchins or really known what he was advocating, have asked: Why haven't there been more like him? Why are there no such inspiring figures today? Why are presidents the pusillanimous ciphers that Kerr describes rather than leaders speaking from a bully pulpit on the crucial issues confronting the larger society as well as on the great questions of education? Other, still earlier presidents are of course also singled out as exemplars who sadly have not been reincarnated—the founders and leaders of the research universities of the later nineteenth and early twentieth century. Kerr's choice of Hutchins was of a unique contemporary in an academic universe that resembled his own more than that of the founders. He saw Hutchins "as the last of the giants in the sense that he was the last of the university presidents who really tried to change his institution and higher education in any fundamental way,"[17] and he admired that attempt.

Clark Kerr was certainly right in saying that Hutchins's critique of higher education in his time was more acerbic than his own. I don't entirely understand his saying that Hutchins paid more dearly than did he for his outspokenness, but perhaps he meant that Hutchins was more embroiled in and scarred by the recurrent battles fought both with his own faculty and with others. But more striking is that Hutchins was so different by temperament and by outlook from Kerr that one is led to speculate as to what the latter saw as their bond beyond the simple fact of speaking out. I think the answer lies in Kerr's recognition of Hutchins's boldness in attempting something he, too, would have liked to try full force; namely, a transforming institutional change in the world of higher education. But Kerr saw also that Hutchins's way could not succeed and would not last.

To my mind, Hutchins's most important contributions were three: (1) to provoke, and to insist on, an intense and ongoing discussion of the nature and purpose of higher education that retains a resonance in current debates; (2) to argue for and work to create a program of general education as the center of liberal learning (that argument, however modified or translated into new language, still remains an active ideal in educational thought); and (3) in the face of major threats, to speak and act in

the cause of academic freedom with courage and with a persua-
sive eloquence that spoke to the vital character of such freedom
in shaping the necessary independence of the university as a
social good. "The university," he wrote,

> is the institution that performs its highest, its unique service to soci-
> ety by declining to do what the society thinks it wants, by refusing
> to be useful in the common acceptance of that word and by insisting
> instead that its task is understanding and criticism. It is a center of
> independent thought. . . .
>   The claim of academic freedom is based on the high and seri-
> ous calling of the academic profession. That calling is to think. A
> university is a center of independent thought. Since it is a center of
> thought, and of independent thought, it is also a center of criticism.
> The freedom of the modern university in a democratic society is
> based not on the remnants of a medieval tradition but on the propo-
> sition that societies require centers of independent thought if they
> are to progress or even to survive.[18]

Clark Kerr surely shared Hutchins's concern with the priority of academic freedom. But while he admired the polemicist's
willingness to take on an assertive critique of higher education
and his boldness in laying out a program of fundamental reform
and while he shared many of Hutchins's concerns, Kerr most
certainly did not share Hutchins's basic outlook or approach.
One might say that Hutchins began with an overriding vision
of what should be and that he was ready to reject or undo history in order to make that ideal a reality, while Kerr began by
accepting the reality of an institution shaped by a history that
could not be denied or undone and then worked to lay out a set
of standards by which its strengths might be harnessed and its
negative effects tempered. In a blurb written in 1989 for Harry

Ashmore's biography of Hutchins, Kerr wrote: "Bob Hutchins was the one person in higher education with whom I disagreed most consistently and at the same time admired the most unreservedly. He always wanted the best and would never settle for the best possible."

There are, of course, other large differences as well. Clark Kerr was writing about the postwar and Cold War university, and from his experience he maintained a perspective that evolved in large part, though not exclusively, from public universities. Hutchins's reflections still assumed the prewar university and his own experience of private institutions. Hutchins's dominant preoccupation was with a philosophy of general education that required integrated curricular and institutional change; Kerr's, that of institutional effectiveness in the service of balancing education and research in a highly pluralistic institution. Hutchins defiantly restated his views in the rather flamboyant book he called *The University of Utopia.* Kerr, in his "Reconsiderations" on *The Uses of the University,* wrote that he regretted not having been able to add a fourth lecture in which he might have indicated "how some of the emerging problems could be solved, how some of the needed changes could best be effectuated." "These lectures would have been more complete," he continued, " . . . if the concluding section had treated with the relation of the university to the eternal search for Utopia."[19]

And just before saying that he should never have given the lectures while president, he wrote:

> One of the frequent criticisms of the original lectures was that I analyzed the university that existed (albeit too ruthlessly) but that I had no vision of what it should be. In that third lecture, however, I certainly had a vision that both placed the university at the center

of the universe and called for it, once again, to become more of a community of people and of interacting intellectuals across the fields of knowledge. I now realize, more than I did then, that this vision was really two visions, and that they are not inherently fully compatible. The former implied larger size and more specialization, and the latter smaller size and more commonality of interests—the best of Berkeley and the best of Swarthmore; but I would still hope that there may be ways to make them more compatible rather than less, although this may be only unguarded utopianism.[20]

In a later addendum, Kerr expressed his ambivalence once again. "I have moved," he wrote, "from guarded optimism to guarded pessimism, but I remain an unguarded Utopian: I believe that we can become 'a nation of educated people,' and that our institutions of higher education will find better ways to associate 'masters and scholars' together in learning communities, as well as better ways for masters to associate in their thinking across, and within, lines of fiercer specialization."[21]

Over decades of study and observation, Clark Kerr came to see the period from roughly 1940 to 1990 as the golden age of American higher education, with the sixties a kind of high point at which the several conditions that could together create progress and reform came to coexist as they could not be expected to do again, combining generous federal funding, expanded access to higher education, and general prosperity. These conditions, Kerr thought, made the sixties a time of great possibility, ripe for the kind of change and experimentation or innovation in education that he was anxious to further. His hopes later rose and flickered by turn as he chronicled cycles of decline even within the half century of gold, marked especially by erosions of resources and federal support and of confidence in higher education. In particular he pointed to the increasing intensity of the problems associated with the multiversity. These problems he identified as the disintegration of the university as a community and the loss of any common understanding of its purpose; a continuing growth of specialization and the intellectual fragmentation of the university that resulted; an increasing weight of external temptations, activities, and pressures in the lives of faculty and their institutions; and a lessening attention to undergraduate education, to the value of the liberal arts, and to the important priorities of teaching. He worried about the state of the academic humanities and the subordination of their role and stature in the curriculum to the sciences and to professional programs in the research university more broadly. He deplored what he saw as a dominant new vocationalism, and he was alarmed by what he viewed as the creeping politicization of the university and the variety of ways in which it was claimed as an instrument of social reform or action. He had been excited by the prospects of reform in the early sixties and believed California's three new campuses, Irvine, San Diego, and Santa Cruz, represented "the most experimental universities in the United States,"[22] and ones that might, in their organization and programs, provide exemplary and influential alternatives to the ills encountered in the multiversity of the day. But he was ultimately saddened by the outcomes that converted these campuses to more conventional patterns of academic organization and behavior, although he thought they had made some small and worthwhile dents in the academic universe.[23]

Altogether, then, *The Uses of the University*, especially in its final form, appears as much a critique as an analysis of the modern research university. Over time, the author's initial hopes of 1963 gave way to a far more skeptical view on the possibility of genuine reform and his judgment that there had been an age of gold to the belief that the worst excesses of that time had not been overcome, indeed had been exacerbated, and that a bleak, if not wholly hopeless, future could be next. Yet he could not entirely abandon his "unguarded Utopianism," even as he asserted that his ideal, a balance of the best of Swarthmore and of Berkeley, was probably unachievable.

Kerr's model research university would counter the overweight of attention to research and graduate training by restoring some sense of unified purpose, within an intellectual community whose members could communicate across the disciplines, to an inevitably fragmented institution of higher learning in which prestige and success had come to be identified too exclusively with research, graduate training, outside funding, and extrauniversity activity and achievement. It would set renewed value on undergraduate education in the liberal arts and on teaching in a curriculum marked by an insistence on breadth and interdisciplinary relationships. At the same time, Utopia U., while achieving the right balance among its diverse parts and interests, would retain the pluralism of the multiversity. There could be, in Kerr's view, no one content of education that was simply right, and there could certainly be no consensus on a single form. For him, the issue was to rebalance and steadily to continue to adapt the university's configuration to the always moving and changing landscape of learning. The goal was not (as in Hutchins's view) to realize a final integration but to establish an equilibrium strong enough to hold and flexible enough to endure over the vagaries of time.

Perhaps most important to observe in Kerr's look at the contemporary research university over so many decades is his conclusion, one that time helped to strengthen, that in the end the
university could not truly be autonomous. He saw the university
increasingly as the product of external historical forces rather
than of deliberate planning and direction and ultimately as having succumbed, a captive in too many ways to some of the less
desirable pressures they entailed.

> There are two great clichés about the university. One pictures it as
> a radical institution, when in fact it is most conservative in its insti-
> tutional conduct. The other pictures it as autonomous, a cloister,
> when the historical fact is that it has always responded, but seldom
> so quickly as today, to the desires and demands of external groups—
> sometimes for love, sometimes for gain, increasingly willingly, and,
> in some cases, too eagerly. The external view is that the university
> is radical; the internal reality is that it is conservative. The internal
> illusion is that it is a law unto itself; the external reality is that it is
> governed by history.[24]

Kerr attributed this basic conservatism to a number of fac-
tors but above all to the faculty's characteristic resistance to
change, and he maintained that change, when it came about,
was more unplanned than planned and that major change[25] had
always been initiated primarily from the outside (and occasionally from the top).[26] The large changes discernible after the
sixties, he believed, had proved it was not educational philosophy and its ideas of reform but the marketplace pure and
simple that would always lead the way. Hence, he believed, the
movement away from the liberal arts to vocational studies and
the dominance of the labor market; hence, too, the university's

enlarged subservience to external sources of funding, whether federal or industrial, that came with strings attached.

At the same time, Kerr believed it was crucial to preserve and enhance the greatest possible independence for the university. All these reflections once again raised in acute form the problems of academic governance and of the role and capacity of academic leadership and what leadership could actually accomplish in the ever more decentralized university, with its complex web of often competing interests and its multiple centers of decision making.

Kerr's thoughts on these issues are far removed from those of Hutchins. Both asked whether, given the structure of university governance and its practice, presidents could exercise sufficient authority to lead at all, or whether their role had become that of arbitrators, bureaucrats, fund-raisers, glad-handers, conveyers of bromides, and petty politicians trying simply to survive in institutions immune to direction or innovation. Such allegations were scarcely new. The tensions inherent in shared authority were born with the university and troubled even the giants whom Hutchins and Kerr rather envied. Thus William Rainey Harper wrote:

[W]hen all is said and done, the limitations of the college president, even when he has the greatest freedom of action, are very great. In all business matters he is the servant of the trustees or corporation; and his views will prevail in that body only in so far as they approve themselves to their good judgment. In educational policy he must be in accord with his colleagues. If he cannot persuade them to adopt his views, he must go with them. It is absurd to suppose that any president, however strong or willful he may be, can force a faculty, made up of great leaders of thought, to do his will. The president, if he has the power of veto, may stand in the way of progress, but he cannot secure forward movement except with the cooperation of those with whom he is associated.[27]

One might see Hutchins and Kerr as representing two sides of an impulse toward educational reform, one uncompromising in his utopianism, the other setting an ideal as a target to be aimed at. Both took on the question of presidential leadership, Hutchins in the name of an integrated unity that would replace an already emergent multiversity and serve a resurrected unity of knowledge, Kerr in an effort to see how leadership might provide a unifying spirit and an impulse to constructive change for an academic space in which a fragmentation of interests, a diversity of ways of knowing, and an inevitable decentralization of power and influence and action had necessarily to be accepted as given conditions. Not how to reverse these but how to create, or re-create, something of a community around them and to establish or restore balance among its different parts, and how to sustain the degree of independence essential to the mission of the university, was the task that Kerr envisaged as the task of academic leadership in the multiversity. The powers he assigned to presidential leadership were those of persuasion and thoughtful spokesmanship. In his view, presidents had to be realists, to understand the contexts of time and place, to choose their initiatives and battles deftly and selectively. This was not for the sake of mere survival and peace but for the cause of expanding and strengthening what he thought the best possibilities of the university and its contribution to the social order. He saw the modern university as in need of reform, and if sometimes tempted by dreams of perfection, his idea of educational reform lay in what could be accomplished in the present to secure, and to render sustainable, incremental changes (they might even be very large ones) that could build strategically on the promise of the multi-university without ignoring its inherent characteristics and without harm to the vibrant spirit that he saw as transforming knowledge and expanding its reach for the greater good in his age. And he wanted to use his office to speak for and to advance the principles and guidelines that should define the higher learning. His notion of Utopia, the merging of the best of Swarthmore and Berkeley, may not sound very utopian; indeed it seems a quite familiar formula. But for Kerr, this ideal had to contend with the realities of a developed multiversity that threatened to suppress or distort its own best features.

The larger questions that preoccupied Kerr—and Hutchins as well—are of course those central to all serious debate over higher education and its institutions. These themes include the definition of the higher learning as such, the purposes for which it should be pursued, the nature of the learning most worth having or creating, the priorities of teaching and research, the responsibilities of institutions of higher education and their members, the conditions required for their effective pursuit, and the relation of such institutions to the larger society. These questions in turn raise those of the fields and studies to be included in the university's work, its defining curriculum, the relation between teaching and research and between graduate or professional and undergraduate education, the nature of authority within the academic community, the strengths and limitations of shared governance, the meaning and value of academic freedom and the imperatives of intellectual autonomy. While the immediate or emerging problems that press on higher education at different times will shape the specific configuration and emphasis given each thread in the complex of issues that have to do with our universities, the larger questions still remain at their center, restated and reargued in the context of new circumstances.

To review the past decades' discussions, criticisms, and proposed programs of reform in the realm of higher education is to see that the questions addressed and the controversies engaged have not been fundamentally new. They have clustered around the same themes voiced earlier about universities but now posed in a new context. We can observe that in the circumstances of today and in the ways in which the problems identified by Kerr, and indeed by Hutchins too, are at once reiterated and given new form. The prevalent sense of deep crisis and uncertainty affecting higher education at present arises not only from the current state of the economy but also from a series of long-developing conditions that have shaped today's universe of higher education and that frame its principal choices. At the same time, the consciousness of massive shifts in the technologies and processes for attaining and transmitting knowledge and learning in a global framework would seem to be pointing the way to a new stage in the life, and in the idea, of universities even beyond the multiversity, and yet that future appears still clouded and obscure.

To speak very broadly, there have been from the outset two somewhat contrasting ideas attached to the American research university: that of the collegiate university and that of the professionalized multiversity. Debates over the nature and purpose and state of the university have tended to go back and forth between these two poles. Similarly there have been two general styles of thinking about the reform of higher education: a single-minded, even utopian kind that begins with an educational philosophy grounded in a vision of an improved or transformed human order; another kind that begins from the structures, contexts, and cultural characteristics of existing institutions and looks toward incremental change adapted to serving more modest but essential goals of the higher learning.

TWO

The University Idea
and Liberal Learning

This chapter undertakes to examine some of the variations played on the themes of an ideal education and an ideal university over time and to ask how these have affected, and continue to affect, our debates over the structures and purposes of liberal learning in a research university. It is quite surprising to find how often Cardinal Newman's *The Idea of a University* is still invoked in writing about higher education. The belief that such an idea should guide the forms and reforms of universities remains seductive even as it would appear challenged by the reality of today's intensely multitasking university. As several commentators have remarked, it often seems as though the only objective research universities possess and assert in common is a commitment to "excellence" or "to be the best."[1] Nonetheless, the search for an ideal both substantive and unifying goes on.

The idea of an idea of a university has a history of its own, a history considerably shorter than that of the university itself. One can perhaps generalize to some conception of a university from the organization and practices and courses of study of the medieval universities and their successors. The specific charters of universities in succeeding eras normally contained some rhetoric as to the reasons for their foundation. But those who later on ascribed an "idea" to the medieval university were using that institution quite unhistorically as an exemplary or symbolic precedent for a complex of ideas born much later in order to assert a continuity that could help lend the weight of apparently unbroken tradition to programmatic aims quite unknown and unthought of in earlier centuries.

The foundation and the institutional structures legislated for the medieval universities had little to do with some articulated vision of higher education or with an appeal to some general idea of a university. The charters issued by ecclesiastical or lay authorities dealt above all with the grants and guarantees of the corporate legal privileges and immunities that these corporations were to enjoy. They were often promulgated at moments of crisis and conflict when clarification was required to protect the rights of faculty and student guilds against encroachment. The statutes of the universities dealt, often in minute detail, with syllabi, degree requirements, teaching obligations and methods, the organization of the faculties, discipline, and academic conduct in general.[2]

The first universities were grounded in the assumptions of Christian doctrine, looking to the education of a learned clergy. Although they did not grow out of a clear idea or plan, they came over recent centuries to represent an idea of a university constantly reconceived and reformulated, appropriated and reappropriated, to the needs, institutions, and aspirations of different times and settings. It was an idea of a community of scholars that stirred people to imagine and depict a sense of the timeless dignity, the enduring worth, the permanence amid the flux and chaos that reigned elsewhere in the world, of the higher learning and its universities. Bologna, Paris, Oxford: these came in a long tradition to stand for the grand accomplishments of medieval learning, for an ideal of the universality and the unity of knowledge, its essential parts ordered in a hierarchy of truth. They stood also for the international character of learning and for a community that transcended boundaries to constitute a larger republic of learning. Their corporate privileges were seen to constitute the fundamental autonomies and freedoms found requisite for the academic world. Their degrees gave life and authority to the profession of teaching and scholarship and to the other learned professions.

Such is the highly generalized image of the ancient and time-less university, of a community of scholars, that has emerged and reemerged in the Western tradition and its literature. The ideas associated with that image have taken on quite different meanings, and shades of meaning, and quite different embodi-ments at different times. The history of the idea of the idea of the university is one of continuing reinterpretation, in which the strongly felt need to assert a continuity with the past confronts the project of giving new life and form and purpose to the higher learning under circumstances quite remote from that past. The past was continually cited to legitimize later ideas, and it was continually altered and given a modern face by doing so.

In the universities of the late Middle Ages the dominant fac-ulties were those of theology, law, and medicine. The faculties of the arts stood at the lowest rung of the curricular hierarchy; their principal role was to prepare and certify students for such higher study by ensuring their mastery of Latin and acquaintance with a set of common texts in the basic liberal arts very narrowly defined.[3] Thus the medieval university was essentially an institution of professional training and advanced scholarship. The liberal arts provided a means to the higher learning, not an educational ideal valuable in its own terms. In effect, the professional university preceded the collegiate one. And the linking of a robust liberal arts tradition to the university arose not from within but initially from outside the universities of the early modern era.

In the real Utopia, to coin an oxymoron, that is, in Thomas More's *Utopia* of 1516, there were no universities. Although all citizens of Utopia, men and women alike, enjoyed the benefits of an excellent liberal education, there is no indication that they established colleges for that purpose or ever received or had need of advanced degrees. The citizens had access to daily public lectures, but attendance carried no course credit. The Utopians even had a designated class of learned people whose special aptitudes for intellectual activity exempted them from ordinary labor so that they might spend their time in reading and scholarship, but these intellectuals were not university professors. It was, however, from this class that governors, diplomats, magistrates, clergy, and other leaders were selected.

More's Utopians set a very high value on the life of the mind and made its continuing cultivation throughout life a principal objective of their social organization. They possessed and acted on a common philosophy of education. It was, quite naturally, utopian, as philosophies of education tend to be. Their ideal of education looked to the liberal arts. Its curriculum was predominantly humanistic (literature, philosophy, ethics, history, rhetoric, and language) while including an element of natural science and a touch of physical education. At its center lay a distinct picture of the kind of person and citizen such education was intended to mold and a clear conviction as to what knowledge was worth having and why. Here we may note several characteristics of Utopian education. The first is that the Utopian defined essential knowledge as mastering already existing truths rather than as a process of making new and accumulating discoveries that went beyond the inheritance of the past. The second is that the manner of achieving such knowledge was essentially text based; it was to take place through the recovery and understanding of the works of classical antiquity. Finally, the reading of such texts was an education in the subjects regarded as together encompassing a unity in which all were interrelated and in which each subject of the liberal arts represented a particular approach to the same set of basic truths.

This humanist vision of education shapes the culture of Utopia. It represents the humanists' alternative to what they believed was a misguided and useless, even harmful, kind of intellectual activity dominating the contemporary university system. The humanists of the Renaissance stood for an ideal of education, initially intended for the schools, that over time came to shape an idea of the collegiate university and its function in training the individual of general competence, the thoughtful citizen, the cultivated person. They felt themselves on the defensive against a university culture that they thought directly opposed to their ideals. This they saw as the culture of scholasticism, an approach to learning and scholarship that the humanists deplored as "merely" academic and overly specialized, as taking refuge in an esoteric jargon and a pedantic, trivializing mode of logic to discuss questions or to rationalize phenomena that had nothing to do with what they believed should really matter. This picture of scholasticism was in many ways a caricature, but the constructed stereotype offered a target against which to argue their own ideas. Learning, they believed, should have to do with probing the great questions of human life, with the molding of human character, and with understanding and strengthening the possibilities of human society. The liberal arts, they thought, should be the basis of such learning; learning should have a moral purpose. And the liberal arts should form not simply a general education preparatory to the professional studies emphasized at the universities; they should represent an education in itself valuable to all no matter what way of life its students might pursue, an education in which learning was translated into positive and active practice and conduct, whether of the citizen and participant in public life, of the private individual seeking both cultivation and ethical conduct, or of the scholar, philosopher, and teacher. Knowledge should have to do with human life and how it should be lived, not with spinning out abstractions remote from the concerns of life in the world.

More used his imaginary state to depict a model society against which to contrast and criticize his own contemporary universe, a model embodying the standards and virtues to which an ideal society should aspire and thereby revealing the evils and shortcomings of the Europe of his day. In urging a radical reform of its institutions, he wanted to demonstrate not just how far from perfection, but how far even from a basic standard of the good, he found the corrupted world of his own day. The institutions and conduct and culture of Utopia present an exact counterpart to a world found in urgent need of a reformed system of education.

And so More joined the ranks of those for whom to speak of education, and what education should be about and for, is to lay out a vision of utopia. Addressing the vice-chancellor and faculty of the University of Oxford in 1518, More wrote that while "one could not expect the whole crowd of academics to possess wisdom, temperance, and humility," he must warn them that the "decay of learning" must be prevented, "and learning will perish if the university continues to suffer from the contentions of lazy idiots, and the liberal arts are allowed to be made sport of with impunity."[4]

There is surely something familiar about the arguments I have been summarizing. I will pass over More's unkind remarks on the character of academics and their disputes and point rather to the larger issue: here we have entered a recurrent debate over the best kind of education and the best kind of knowledge, the best method of acquiring and using that knowledge, the purpose and value of learning, and the ends toward which it should be designed.

In these debates the exponent of a particular program tends, whether explicitly or not, to make certain assumptions: about the essential nature and ultimate ends of human life, about the state of society and its needs, about the kind of person the educated individual should become, about the kind of future that person will inhabit. And the utopian impulse may envisage a truly altered, perhaps perfected future, one that can be realized in significant part by a scheme of education.

Much discussion of education is utopian in these senses. Its commentaries usually begin by depicting a crisis, arguing that something is fundamentally amiss or in decay in the state of education. In assuming that things are generally getting worse, it assumes also that things were once brighter in a golden age from which the present has declined.

Thomas More and his fellow humanists set a utopian education in the liberal arts against what we might call vocational or professional training, a general education against specialized or technical learning, and education for life against intellectual activity undertaken for ends that were in their opinion scarcely relevant to the goals of building ethical character and active commitment to the public good. In protesting the scholarship pursued at the universities, they were making their statement about the knowledge most worth having and asserting that a liberal education could be a means to the reform and sustenance of a decayed society and a path toward acquiring a genuine wisdom in place of an abstruse and worthless learning.

As the humanists' program came to penetrate the university faculties of the arts and as the demand for lay higher education grew, the collegiate idea began to grow within the universities but without yet creating a new idea of a university per se, for the universities retained their essentially medieval organization and its priorities. Increasingly, in the early modern age of religious warfare, the universities became the homes of endless theological controversy and pervasive orthodoxy, and there arose a kind of new scholasticism that permeated the humanistic as well as the theological domain. The goals of humanistic scholarship became, so to speak, more academic; its spirit more closed and defensive of tradition as such. It is not surprising that the great intellectual revolutions of the seventeenth and early eighteenth century were not destined, in the main, to emerge out of the universities.

To the extent that one might search for the idea of the university as one centering on the liberal arts, then, it is only partially to be found in the universities of early modern Europe, despite the huge influence humanism exercised on learning in the faculties of the arts in that era and despite the almost sovereign role of the colleges at Oxford and Cambridge. It was to be some time before the liberal arts idea would hold a vital dominance in the idea of a university. When it did come to do so, the arguments for liberal learning retained much of their original humanist flavor.

In his *Idea of a University*, Cardinal Newman gave lasting language to the conviction that a university should embody an idea, a set of beliefs about the knowledge most worth having, the kind of person education should seek to develop, and the kind of institution in which that education should go forward.[5] He proposed an idea of a university founded in a largely traditional conception of the liberal arts with the humanities at their center, one that excluded research, locating the discovery and advancement of knowledge in separate academies and confining the university to the function of teaching. What has continued to appeal about his view and is constantly recalled, while being pulled and stretched almost out of recognition to fit a very different academic environment, is his insistence on a broad or general education in the liberal arts in an institution dedicated to a civilizing cause and looking rather like an idealized model of an Oxford college. It is striking to observe the ways in which Newman's language has been invoked to speak for an idea of American liberal education and of the American university very differently conceived and constituted from the education and institution that Newman himself envisaged.[6]

It is sometimes overlooked that Newman was also preoccupied with the theme, now restated in a nineteenth-century version, of the relation between faith and reason, religious commitment and worldly learning. That of course had been the central concern of medieval thought in its speculations and controversies over the justification, scope, and uses of secular studies in a universe of higher revealed truth. His goal was to find the means by which the training of the mind and the unity of liberal learning ("universal knowledge"), understood as a good in itself, could be given life and power in a way that would be congruent also with the prescriptions of faith and obedience.[7]

Thus Newman's "idea" of a university has significant associations with the past while simultaneously assimilating and expanding a collegiate ideal of his own time that he placed at the heart of a "true" university. And his "true" university, asserting both the unity of knowledge and the value of learning for its own sake, represented an idea in opposition to the kind of university that Newman saw elsewhere beyond the ancient foundations of Oxford and Cambridge.[8] Its first object was intellectual. Newman's university was antiutilitarian in essence, but it promised practical social benefit as well by training "good members of society," educated gentlemen who would lead and enhance the culture of their society.[9]

This collegiate ideal stands in contrast to the conception of a university given shape in the founding of Wilhelm von Humboldt's University of Berlin earlier in the century.[10] The idea was that of a graduate university rooted in a liberal humanistic philosophy that looked to a breadth of basic scholarship whose different parts together illuminated a coherent universality of thought and learning to be expanded and pursued for their own sake at the highest intellectual level. Humboldt's idea of a university celebrated an ideal of *Wissenschaft*, of a learning and cultivation both broad and deep, with research carried out to extend knowledge itself through new discovery and interpretation, and with students initiated into the grand tradition of learning through advanced study in a given field. The institutional form of this university required academic freedom for professor and student alike, so that the goal of intellectual creativity, the following of rigorous investigation and analysis wherever these might lead, could be fully encouraged and realized.

Such freedom now became an essential dimension of the idea of a university. The ideal of intellectual freedom came not to replace but to loom over that of the liberties provided by the corporate privileges and legal immunities granted the medieval universities and their successors. Institutional autonomy now became an essential means for securing and sustaining the end of intellectual freedom at the university's center. Such corporate freedom was vital to the university's main work, that of scholarship, research, and advanced training carried on by its individual members.

This idea of a university dedicated primarily to research and graduate education, an institution in which knowledge might be searched out and advanced unfettered by utilitarian considerations or by the orthodoxies of other traditions, or by the pressures of state control, or by the demands of elementary collegiate instruction, came to have a powerful hold on those who saw the nineteenth-century college or university as moribund institutions badly in need of reform. Nowhere was this influence more compelling than in the case of those American academic figures who spent some time, especially in the mid-nineteenth century, at German universities.

By that day, the course of American higher education had been set toward pluralism and decentralization, with a mix also of public and private.[11] There were those who, in the early days of the Republic, had argued for a federal university that would train the nation's future leaders and help create and instill a common culture, but that was not to be (outside the military academies). The state of private higher education generally reflected its origins in religious tradition, a sectarian spirit, and a narrowly collegiate curriculum.

The university movement of the late nineteenth century, as it gained momentum, conceived an idea of a university quite removed from the dominant collegiate model, with its self-conception as the home of inherited learning and its transmission. It advocated a new focus on scholarly investigation and discovery, a wide embrace of all the emerging and newly created fields of knowledge and study, including modern languages and literatures and, above all, the introduction of science and scientific research. The reform of higher education would entail the transformation of already existing colleges into universities and the founding of entirely new ones. The old collegiate model was now vigorously challenged as failing to produce truly educated graduates, as a thin and atrophied form of rote learning of little use, as unsuited to meeting the significant needs and interests of a new age, and as ludicrously unresponsive to the requirements and developments of the contemporary world.

The old humanist view of the liberal arts was giving way to very different ideas of their content and educational role. No longer did they assign overriding authority to tradition, to the legacy of the past. They looked instead to the authority of science and to the belief in an infinitely expanding universe of discovery.[12] The intellectual revolution by which the authority of scientific criteria of truth and knowledge came to dominance in the universities had profound consequences for all academic fields, not least the humanities, once the reigning subjects of the liberal arts. The liberal arts were no longer simply grounded in texts thought to contain an essential unity of truth. They found their focus rather in the various methods of inquiry associated with disparate categories of learning. The classical texts might represent important sources of culture, but they were to be given critical scrutiny. The modern view sees the liberal arts as, literally, liberating, as freeing the mind from unexamined opinions and assumptions to think independently and exercise critical judgment, to question conventional doctrines and inherited claims to truth, to gain some skill in analysis and some capacity to deal with complexity, to embrace a certain skepticism in the face of dogma, and to be open to many points of view. These ideas came increasingly to shape the directions of liberal education in the universities and colleges.

An idea of a university as comprehending a whole universe of learning at every level now became the distinctive type, albeit with many variations, for the American university. It is common to see the development of the American university as combining the two strands of an English collegiate tradition and a German research model. But this interpretation should not be overstated. Despite the influence that each exerted, such models could not have been simply grafted onto the diverse institutions already present in a distinctive American culture. The role of land grant universities, for example, necessarily had to take account of the direct services to which their public supporters and beneficiaries might be entitled. American universities, from the outset, tended to view themselves as endowed with more than a single purpose. In essence, the multiversity was born already with the universities of the late nineteenth century.

As early as 1851, Henry Tappan, soon to be president of the University of Michigan, wrote as follows: "How simple the idea of a university. An association of eminent scholars in every department of human investigation; together with the books embodying the results of human investigation and thinking, and all the means of advancing and illustrating knowledge. . . . How simple the law which is to govern this association!—That each member as a thinker, investigator, and teacher shall be a law unto himself, in his own department."

Tappan cited as his models the University of Paris, the German universities, and the universities of England "before they were submerged in the Colleges." He called them "Cyclopaedias of education." His idea of a university placed comprehensiveness of knowledge, including practical learning, at its center. The university was to be a beacon of civilization for the entire society and an instrument for elevating the nation's culture. It would possess every good, from libraries and laboratories to art museums and botanical gardens, that could conduce to the preservation and advancement of the sciences, letters, and arts. There would be no conflict between the scientific and the humanistic or between knowledge pursued for its own sake and applied knowledge. The intellectual and the utilitarian would exist in harmony. Tappan expressed an enormous faith in the power of scholarship and trained intelligence to work progressively for the greater good. He linked his idea of this new university to those of the old world, both medieval and modern, suggesting that the medieval university itself embodied such an idea. But his eclectic university had little to do with Paris or Oxford or Berlin. He took the several purposes assigned to universities over their history—the pursuit of pure learning for its own sake, the service of social and civic ends, the development of individual capacity and virtue—and gathered them together as part and parcel of a single space. That space looks strikingly like a multiversity.[13]

Charles William Eliot of Harvard took office in 1869 with a clear idea in mind as to what his university should seek to become. His vision was grounded in the elective system. For Eliot an elective system, replacing the confining requirements of the traditional common curriculum and expanding the fields of learning to include the modern sciences, would in effect make possible research and scholarship and advanced training in a university environment that provided the greatest possible freedom for its individual members in the pursuit of knowledge and that assumed a close relation between teaching and research. "The largest effect of the elective system," he wrote, "is that it makes scholarship possible, not only among undergraduates, but among graduate students and college teachers." And again: "As long as our teachers regard their work as simply giving so many courses for undergraduates, we shall never have first-class teaching. . . . If they have to teach graduate students as well as undergraduates, they will regard their subjects as infinite, and keep up that constant investigation which is necessary for first-class learning."[14]

Eliot's university at the end of his long term, as Oscar Handlin has written, had merged an inherited ideal of liberal education with that of scholarship, "ever evolving as knowledge accumulated. Tradition yielded to science as the source of authority."[15]

It is in that transition from tradition to science as the source of intellectual authority in the world of learning that the modern idea of the university came to be born. There took place a decisive shift from an emphasis on inherited learning and its preservation and transmission to focus on the freedom that had necessarily to accompany the conviction that knowledge was an open and infinite area of new discovery, with multiple paths of entry. The methods of the sciences, too, gained an ascendancy and an influence on all the disciplines that was to change the organization of the university forever. The rapid professionalization and specialization in the fields of learning and inquiry, the new emphasis on graduate education and certification through the Ph.D. degree as a growing condition for membership in the professoriate, the creation of academic departments around the fields of specialization and of professional organizations around the disciplines—all this created an academic profession and a new set of expectations in the world of higher education, whether in the universities that were built on the foundations of existing colleges or in those that were founded anew.

In 1892 a new university opened its doors in Chicago. Its president, William Rainey Harper, had started by writing down an entire blueprint covering every detail of its program and organization. "I have a plan for the organization of the University," he wrote,

> which will revolutionize College and University work in this country. It is "bran splinter new," and yet as solid as the ancient hills. . . .
> It is expected . . . that the university idea is to be emphasized. It is proposed to establish, not a college, but a university. . . . It is only

the man who has made investigation who can teach others how to investigate. . . . Promotion of younger men . . . will depend more largely upon the results of their work as investigators than upon the efficiency of their teaching, although the latter will by no means be overlooked. In other words it is proposed in this institution to make the work of investigation primary, the work of giving instruction secondary.[16]

Harper's university, sometimes referred to by contemporary doubters as "Harper's Bazaar," envisaged not only a range of graduate and professional schools, but a major program of extension and continuing education and a university press as integral to its mission. His ideas did not appeal to everyone, and five years later Harper replied to his critics:

> There has been a feeling on the part of some that the institution has not conserved sufficiently the traditions of the past. These friends, if they are friends, have forgotten that it is in the nature of a university to occupy the advanced positions; that a university, if it will justify its name, must be a leader of thought, and that however cautious and conservative may be the policy of such an institution, the great majority of men are accustomed to follow far behind. It cannot be expected that such will sympathize with those whose responsibilities force them to the forefront in the great and continuous conflict of thought.[17]

It was also in 1896 that Princeton celebrated its 150th anniversary and officially declared itself a university. The faculty speaker for this event was Professor Woodrow Wilson. He delivered an address that could almost have been a reply to Harper's words in a speech that deplored the loss of tradition and its stabilities to the aggressive force of a new and unsettling academic environment. Wilson struck at the spirit of scientism and the sterile academic specialization he thought had invaded the higher learning:

> I am much mistaken if the scientific spirit of the age is not doing us a great disservice, working in us a certain degeneracy. Science has bred in us a spirit of experiment and a contempt for the past.
>
> Can anyone wonder ... that I ask for the old drill, the old memory of times gone by, the old schooling in precedent and tradition, the old keeping of faith with the past, as a preparation for leadership in days of social change? We have not given science too big a place in our education, but we have made a perilous mistake in giving it too great a preponderance in method in every other branch of study. We must make the humanities human again; must recall what manner of men we are; must turn back once more to the region of practicable ideals.[18]

Wilson's words remind us that, from the outset, the emerging universities of the late nineteenth century attracted fierce debate over the relative positions of the sciences and the humanities, of academic inquiry and liberal learning, in their work of education and research. The driving norms for the standards of research, whatever the field, were meant to be "scientific," investigatory, critical, professional, and disciplinary. To some extent these norms had already transformed humanistic scholarship as the organization of departments and graduate study and the growing specialization of the disciplines swept up the humanities as well.

In opposition, there were those who lamented these developments as threatening to kill the spirit and the purpose of a university culture that should find meaning and worth in humanistic roots and goals. They grieved over what they saw as the disintegration of a once-unified curriculum and deplored the attention and deference accorded the natural sciences and newer social sciences, as well as the mounting professionalization and specialization that affected both teaching and the growing status of research. They believed that a general or liberal education was in peril of succumbing to the practical and scientific and that the prospects for the universities as beacons of a civilizing mission were in sharp decline.[19]

In yet other reactions to the new university culture, William James spoke out against what he called the "Ph.D. Octopus" as a specious advertising gimmick dreamed up by universities to raise their prestige and image in competition with their peers. He saw no reason why this new kind of certification should be a requirement for the professoriate. And Thorstein Veblen saw universities, early in the twentieth century, as falling prey to destructively corporate and commercial values. Arguing passionately against the commercialized university, he defined the "idea" of a university as follows: "A university is a body of mature scholars and scientists, the 'faculty,'—with whatever plant and other equipment may incidentally serve as appliances for their work."[20] The university of his day, in his view, had veered off course by falling into the hands of businessmen and being subjected to management by business principles and practices that corrupted and distorted the true ends of an institution that should be devoted to the advancement of learning per se. A fierce critic of what he found an offensively childish and anti-intellectual collegiate culture, he favored an institution dedicated purely to graduate study and research as the only type of a "real" university.

It is striking that so many themes familiar from earlier times continued to resonate through the late twentieth century. The academy was taking on a new look and a new energy in the post–World War II era. It was felt urgent to review liberal arts curricula in the light of the experience of the war and its aftermath and the aspirations that might now be realized for a promising new future. Discussions of liberal education gave special prominence to the project of training educated citizens who would lead and strengthen democracy in the new era and to the new internationalism that had developed with America's expanded role in the world. A common engagement with the heritage of Western civilization, it was argued, should be placed at the center of the curriculum, allowing reflection on the core values, basic institutions, and foundational traditions of a society that had become ever more conscious of their importance as it fought against their possible destruction. A general education should offer an introduction to the greatest and most influential accomplishments and works of philosophy, literature, and the arts, together with some exposure to other cultures and ways of thought, some understanding of modern science and its implications, some study of the methods and leading ideas of the social sciences, and some introduction to the larger movements of history that had culminated in the postwar world.

This view of general education, in its preoccupation with achieving meritocracy and looking toward the enhancement of educated citizenship and of cultural unity, was rather different from Columbia's primarily humanistic and historical Contemporary Civilization program, the product of an earlier postwar period, or from the core curriculum championed by Robert Maynard Hutchins, with its metaphysical underpinnings and faith in the unity of knowledge. The so-called Red Book, written by a committee of Harvard faculty under the title

General Education in a Free Society, put forward its case for general education as the basis for liberal learning in a democracy and as a corrective to both vocationalism and the excesses of specialization. "In recent times," the authors wrote, "the question of unity has become insistent. We are faced with a diversity of education which . . . works against the good of society by helping destroy the common ground of training and outlook on which any society depends." "It is impossible," they continued, "to escape the realization that our society . . . rests on common beliefs and that a major task of education is to perpetuate them." But it was also important, they added, for a liberal education "to reconcile this necessity for common belief with the equally obvious necessity for new and independent insights leading to change."[21]

Harvard never in fact adopted the Red Book's recommendations in their entirety, and its guidelines were generally more praised than practiced. For most institutions, distribution requirements rather than a common core of courses designed specifically as general education offerings became the order of the day. But the Red Book continued for a long time to be read as a canonical text for the definition of a liberal education as of a general education; indeed, the two were often conflated.

Conditions change and fashions change. Pressure from both faculty and students for a loosening of restrictions and a greater freedom of choice in what to teach and what to study—in short, something like a fuller elective system—soon led to curricular changes in many institutions that had adopted basic requirements. In response there arose widespread criticism of what some feared an alarming disintegration of standards and a loss of educational purpose. In addition, the rapid expansion of universities in the postwar era caused growing anxiety that undergraduate education was being subordinated to research and graduate training in the priorities of higher education, that there might be indeed an inherent conflict between teaching and research, and that respect for teaching and any hope for curricular coherence were losing out. The utopian project of reconstructing a "unity of knowledge" among a community of scholars and learners seemed to such critics to have given way to the research-oriented priorities of the professionalized and inevitably splintered multiversity.

The wave of radicalism that swept the campuses from the mid-sixties into the early seventies intensified the demand for students' freedom of choice and the elimination of requirements. The new revolutionaries condemned traditional liberal arts programs with such epithets as "elitist" and "irrelevant," calling for a system of higher education directed toward the priorities of transforming the immediate social and political order, of helping to introduce sweeping reform in a society urgently in need of an ethos and of new institutional arrangements that could activate the goals of equality, peace, and justice. The radical view found current forms of liberal education hopelessly removed from the world, mired in the obsolete ideas of a discredited past, too closely allied with and supportive of the status quo of privilege and power. These utopians did not, however, want to abandon the institution of the university they condemned so harshly; they wanted rather to remake it from an inhumane and authoritarian institution serving the powers that be into an ideal community and to recast its liberal arts curricula into an education for social action and for liberation from the weight of the past.

The relatively short but intense period of campus upheavals stimulated renewed controversy over the role and governance and purposes of universities as such, as well as over the nature of a liberal education. The legacy of thinking about the institution as a kind of ideal community did not necessarily imply an activist or single political position, let alone a single curriculum. Nor did the opposing view that reasserted the ideal of the university as a neutral space in which the fullest and freest expression of divergent ideas would effectively encourage and protect the disinterested pursuit of learning and where teaching and research would reinforce one another. Nonetheless, over time, debates over the functions of universities and the best form of liberal education came to take on a significant political coloration.

The conflicts that ensued demonstrate well how thinking about education is inevitably to be addressing a whole complex of other concerns as well. The critique of education is a way of identifying what is seen as sadly imperfect in the society, culture, and direction of the contemporary world. An ideal of education proposed as at least a partial solution to its current defects must be also a statement of possibility about the future (and often, too, a statement about a better and romanticized past) and about preparing people to take effective control of that future. Debates over what the ideal might look like will arise from differing conceptions of human purpose, of the social order, of the knowledge most worth having and the uses of such knowledge. Finally, these debates have over the centuries, and despite large changes of historical context, demonstrated some common and recurrent themes. One such theme is the claim on behalf of reform that existing programs are "irrelevant," "useless," "incoherent," "merely academic," or, still worse, instruments of control and oppression; all this implies an urgent impulse to reform the larger world as well. Another is the contrasting claim that existing programs fail to provide a solid foundation of a learning good in itself, respectful of a long tradition woven into the culture we inherit and beneficial to both individual and society. Without necessarily embracing the status quo, this claim implies a different set of judgments about the direction and the needs of the social order.

As we have seen, the liberal arts have been invoked on all sides of these disputes. What emerged as to some extent new in the sixties and beyond was a belief that the university or college itself should represent a kind of utopian community, not of the ivory tower removed from its surroundings, but of an exemplary counterpoint to the world out there, not only in its educational program, but in its internal policies and social organization as well. This, in whatever form, has become yet another idea of a university, and one that links the idea of what is to be taught, and why it is to be taught in a liberal arts program, very closely to the purposes of social reform.

Since the sixties what we call the liberal arts have again undergone large changes. Their advocates may agree in their opposition to what is called "pre-professional" education, but they remain otherwise strongly divided. In our recent past those divisions became part of a wider series of controversies stimulated in part by epistemological debates over the possibility of asserting certain or objective knowledge; by the rise of minority, feminist, and gender studies and increasing attention to cultural and comparative studies; by the accelerated pace of discovery in the sciences and the enhanced position of the sciences in the university world; by the growing awareness of a global society; and by the transformative impact of new technologies.

The standard questions repeatedly posed about liberal education continue to be asked: What is its value and purpose? How can or should it prepare students for the "real" world, for the challenges of the future? What form of the liberal arts can best meet our society's need for trained intelligence and constructive citizenship? To what degree should we think of a liberal education as a good in itself that requires no utilitarian justification?

But we have heard questions and arguments not quite so old as well, for example, about the study of Western civilization or about the existence of a canon of works, or a tradition of the past, however flexibly conceived and brought up to date, that might shape a general foundation of learning for anyone who claims to be educated. Is there, it is asked, a hierarchy of significant learning that can guide the choices to be made in structuring an educational program? Or should one emphasize rather the difficulty of making such judgments and assume an essential relativity of cultures, thought, and beliefs? If so, what best set of options can be found to comprise a liberal education and by what criterion should these be chosen? and to what end? In selecting what is to be taught, should not more attention now be paid to the global character of our world, to the issues of diversity, to groups and subjects previously ignored or marginalized, and to the social consequences of higher education as it is practiced?

Historians have an annoying habit of telling you that everything has happened before, that there is nothing new under the sun. In the same breath, they will tell you that everything is different, indeed unique in the annals of time. We have seen that certain questions and patterns have remained in many ways constant over the centuries and that a way of thinking about the liberal arts was in fact bequeathed to the modern age by much earlier predecessors. But it is true also that an apparently similar vocabulary can mean quite different things in the context of historical and intellectual changes that cause us to ask the old questions anew in the light of our own circumstances and dilemmas.

As one significant example, the understanding of what constitutes the humanities has altered with the increasingly professionalized character of scholarship in the humanistic disciplines, with the emergence of new theoretical models for interpretation and criticism, and also with the enlargement of content included at least in part under the humanists' umbrella: popular culture; minority-, ethnic-, and gender-related subjects; and the large interdisciplinary category "cultural studies." There has appeared a growing gap between the intellectual preoccupations of many academic humanists and the expectations of those who may see in the specialized humanities a kind of scholasticism with its own arcane language, not a path to the exploration of the perennial questions of life and history that was once envisaged at the core of a philosophy of liberal learning.

Over the past decades, those who advocate that liberal education begin with an introduction to principal aspects of the Western humanistic tradition have often come to be seen as reactionaries taking a posture of social conservatism. Critics of the state of contemporary education have tended to see critical theory in the humanities and multiculturalism in the curriculum as fashions that signal the rise of political correctness and its evils and as destroying shared standards of quality and judgment. Those critics have condemned theories that deny certainty in the meaning of texts or in judgments as to their relative merits.

They have argued against the view that language is arbitrary and culture the reflection of power and its relations, maintaining that this teaching has led to a radical relativism that could eliminate the possibility of a culture based on reason. For their opponents on the other side, these attacks have been seen as reflecting an unwillingness to understand new theoretical constructs or accept new styles of scholarship that have opened important new horizons or to respect ideas that might challenge an outmoded and "elitist" norm of education and expose the parochial biases, paternalistic assumptions, and Western triumphalism informing an agenda aimed at maintaining the dominance of an unsatisfactory status quo.[22]

It is important to emphasize that there is no one school of the humanities. And I have given much too simplistic an account of disputations far more complicated and varied. But this tendentious summary of wars over the state of the humanities in the curriculum and in academic scholarship, and their meaning for the contemporary condition of education and culture, points to the ways in which those oppositions have tended generally to be perceived. The echoes of these battles still reverberate even as they have been moderating in fact.

The history of Western culture has been a history of criticism and debate, of constant questioning, argument, and reinterpretation. Our tradition is marked by a never-ending dialogue of sharply diverging voices. It is a tradition intensely self-critical and intensely self-conscious, characteristically interested in coming to know other cultures in part as a way to define its own, to question its own assumptions and enlarge its own experience. It is a tradition that has in fact shaped the basic life and vigor of the university itself, at every level.[23]

My own belief is that an introduction to some of the seminal ideas that characterize our culture is an essential part of a liberal education and not an act of political indoctrination. I do not believe that this "privileges" Western culture above others or asserts a stance of moral superiority. I do not imagine that to insist on studying Western civilization means adherence to one narrative or to one group or to one way of thought. I would certainly require the study of another culture once the student has learned something of, and therefore been able to achieve some distance from, his or her own. For a liberal education must seek to engender a mental framework and spirit in which one can to some degree overcome the limitations of one's own location in time and place and ways of thought to gain some understanding of other minds and worlds.

Here to the point are some words of Irving Howe, a fierce old-fashioned radical, looking back on his experience of liberal education at City College of New York:

> Knowledge of the past, we felt, could humanize by promoting distance from ourselves and our narrow habits, and this could promote critical thought. Even partly to grasp a significant experience or literary work of the past would require historical imagination, a sense of other times, which entailed moral imagination, a sense of other ways. It would create a kinship with those who had come before us, hoping and suffering as we have, seeking through language, sound, and color to leave behind something of enduring value.

He went on to say, "Serious education must assume, in part, an adversarial stance toward the very society that sustains it—a democratic society makes the wager that it is worth supporting a culture of criticism. But if that criticism loses touch with the heritage of the past, it becomes weightless, a mere compendium of momentary complaints."[24]

Today other concerns, particularly ones arising out of economic crisis, are supplanting those of the "culture wars" at center stage. A new wave of educational debate has arisen from the questions of access to and of the costs and desirable outcomes of higher education. Here, once again, the humanities will find themselves on the defensive against a strengthened utilitarianism and against the background of the long decline of confidence in the value accorded the enterprise of liberal learning.

A survey published last spring by the Higher Education Research Institute at the University of California, Los Angeles, found that the proportion of professors who believe it very important to teach undergraduates to become "agents of social change" is substantially larger than the proportion who believe it important to teach students the classic works of Western civilization. The director of the institute said that this large gap (57.8 to 34.7 percent) reflects a shift from the abstract to the practical. "The notion of a liberal education as a set of essential intellectual skills is in transition," she says. "It's also about social and personal responsibility, thinking about one's role in society, and creating change."[25]

If she is right, then the collegiate idea of the university has moved yet further from its traditional center in the liberal arts. The state of the liberal arts is being shaped not only by the vocational preoccupations of the moment but also by an agenda that emphasizes the student's total experience rather more than his or her intellectual development as the point of a college education. At the same time, the work of the universities has moved toward still greater specialization and subspecialization in the disciplines of learning; even the current emphasis on encouraging more interdisciplinary programs is to some degree an opening to new and indeed interesting and fruitful forms of specialization. In addition, universities have in recent decades taken on even more functions outside their immediate academic mandates than Henry Tappan ever dreamed of.

I would argue that in this world of specialization and fragmented attention, the liberal arts become even more important, both to provide some core of a general education and of a broad cultural perspective valuable in themselves and for the capacities of mind they help develop and to enrich the study and understanding of the specialties themselves. To quote Jaroslav Pelikan: "The difference between good scholarship and great scholarship is, as often as not, the general preparation of the scholar in fields other than the field of specialization. It is general preparation that makes possible that extra leap of the imagination and analogy by which scholarship moves ahead."[26]

THREE

Uses (and Misuses)
of the University Today

Today's most familiar model of the university remains that of Kerr's version of the multiversity as it had emerged in the postwar era. That university is essentially the product of the alliance forged between government funding and university research, of the Cold War and the conviction that research and training could strengthen America's competitive position, of the G.I. Bill and its transforming effects on the college population, of the baby boom, of the economic boom of the 1960s, of the women's and civil rights movements, of the quickening expansion of knowledge and new technologies, of the impact of globalization and economic competition. The growth and proliferation of higher education in the immediate postwar period were rooted in an exuberant faith in what education might do to expand the promise of a more truly democratic society, one that would open an inclusive access to higher education for more and more young people to ensure a genuine meritocracy, one in which the "endless frontiers" of knowledge and its discovery would push ahead to the benefit of all. Teaching and research would go hand in hand to strengthen the potential of higher education, a potential to be realized in practical as well as intellectual contributions offering powerful support to the health and progress of the larger society.

Since the postwar period of expanded development of universities in numbers and size, in programs and research, a time so often referred to as the "golden age" of the American university, much has happened to moderate the brightest hopes and complicate the many questions surrounding our universities. Since the late sixties, and partly in consequence of the critiques and movements that then affected higher education and the public's view of higher education, there has arisen widespread skepticism, and often cynicism, about institutions and their promises. Paradoxically the time of radical dissent and its controversies left yet another and, I think, more troubling legacy that has not faded; namely, an ideal of the university or college as a perfect or perfectible society exemplifying all the virtues lacking in the world outside, at peace from its destructive conflicts, but finally a source of social action and reform.

Putting aside for the moment the different conclusions reached by different commentators, it is striking to note how similar were the themes and how strong the nostalgia expressed in discussions of the university during the decades of the late twentieth century. Those decades saw a great outpouring of criticism launched against contemporary higher education and also of controversy over the directions in which it was seen to be heading. They were marked also by a recurrent sense of crisis emanating above all from economic downturns, the vagaries of federal support for science and financial aid, demographic projections that (mistakenly, as it turned out) forecast a significant decline in future college populations, and concerns about the costs and effects of increased regulation.

The sixties played a double role in all this. One part was taken by the image and legacy, or various interpreted legacies, of the era of student protest. The other offered an idealized picture of the golden age of the research university, a time to which each succeeding decade with its burden of problems was compared and found wanting.

The memories of campus conflict associated with the late sixties and early seventies left a strong imprint on the controversies that followed. In many cases, faculty divisions that had sprung up in that era continued for a considerable period to affect the internal academic politics of their institutions. For those who saw radical activism and the institutional responses it provoked as threatening the core values and goals of universities, the fear that these had been compromised perhaps beyond any possibility of restoration became a rallying cry for an assault on what they saw as an alien academic culture transformed by a new irrationalism, an extreme politicization, and a repudiation of intellectual standards. To choose one example: Allan Bloom's *The Closing of the American Mind* is in essence a reflection on his experiences during the period of radical activism at Cornell, an institution that he believed had capitulated to the worst features of a destructive movement. His thinking about universities remained always shaped by his history there, just as his emotional attachment to the Hutchins college remained the foundation for his view of what higher education had once been and still should be. Other critiques that followed his tended also to see the late sixties as the turning point in the decline of American education and culture and to bemoan the passing of a tradition of general education based in the classic texts, achievements, and ideas of Western civilization. While it may seem difficult to argue that such intellectual trends as deconstructionism, for example (the bane of these critics), had anything directly to do with sit-ins and the rest, they saw those developments, together with the emerging curricula of multicultural and gender studies and the attention to policies having to do with affirmative action and such matters as speech and its regulation on campus, as parts of a larger phenomenon that, in their view, found its origins in the politics of the sixties.[1]

With the student revolution and the alienation of radical groups from the institutional patterns and educational directions that a liberal academic center wanted earnestly to reform but that the new left demanded wholly to transform, there came into being an intense and divisive conflict over the sustenance of the basic ethos to which universities had been committed. Its criteria had to do with freedom of research and teaching and speaking in the academy, with the independence of the individual scholar and scientist, with the ideal of the disinterested pursuit of learning, and with the political neutrality that the university required for the robust support of these ends. Believing these imperiled, their defenders saw the time of confrontation as the most serious crisis yet to have afflicted the universities, perhaps still more threatening than the danger posed by McCarthyism. For they recognized that the radical challenge and the anti-intellectualism that marked much of its advocacy arose from within the universities themselves, demanding new missions and new forms of internal governance and holding out a vision of the university increasingly dogmatic in ideological content.

I can remember that well into the 1980s people would ask, with a meaningful look, "Are things pretty quiet on your campus?" By this they apparently intended to inquire as to whether anyone had burned down a building recently or whether my office was being occupied by bearded youths in camouflage garb. Yet at the same time, they seemed a little regretful that student activism had all but disappeared, wishing perhaps that young people would be politically more engaged and less preoccupied with career planning. In any case the persistence of such questions demonstrated how long the dimming shades of the 1960s hung over a public perception of America's campuses.

The vision of the 1960s as the golden age of the research university has had an even longer life. Seen as a time of prosperity and growth and of a seller's market for aspirants to an academic life, a time of ever more generous federal funding for the enterprise of science and for financial aid, and of expanding opportunities for the support of graduate study and important areas of scholarship that would find a home in the now rapidly broadening universe of universities, the era of gold, brief and indeed anomalous as it turned out to be, set expectations that have influenced our universities ever since. The sense of decline in federal support and public favor and of constriction in the academic marketplace has remained a sense of a precipitous falling away from what once was and still ought to be the rightful norm in the world of higher education.[2]

We tend to forget that people of that era did not necessarily think of themselves as living in an age of gold, any more than medieval men considered themselves as living in a Middle Age. In that time the reaction against the prospering multiversity developed in immediate reaction to its apparent success. The flow of federal funding to the universities, justified in the political realm by Cold War competition and its accompanying goals of national security, brought with it issues of classified research, of external regulation and political influence for institutions, as also for the choice and treatment of research topics. It provoked fierce tensions over the opposing claims of basic and applied research and of different fields clamoring for support, as well as concerns over universities becoming part of the "military-industrial complex."

The golden age stimulated Clark Kerr's worst fears as well as his strong sense of what had been accomplished and his hopes for the future. It saw continuing complaints over the disappearance of the idea and reality of a community of scholars; the increasing specialization and fragmentation of knowledge, with the concomitant erosion of faculty loyalty to the institution and its replacement by free agency and an overriding attachment to discipline and individual interest; the perceived subordination of undergraduate attachment to research and the loss of curricular coherence.

The golden age was relatively brief; its effects were lasting. It gave an indelible shape to the research universities we know today. Its legacy was to seal the partnership between federal funding and the university research enterprise and to set strong expectations for the continued growth of higher education in all its dimensions and for the continuing widening of access to its benefits. As the resources for growth then began to slow, as new conflicts and constraints emerged, and as public priorities shifted in some degree to other areas on the nation's agenda, universities experienced a weakening of internal unity, a lowering of public regard, and a heightened exposure to external pressures.

In the decades that followed, those concerned with governance in the academic world came often to say that administrative authority had waned and that faculty had moved away from considering the institution and its welfare as a whole, that constant growth and its companion, decentralization, had set up still further obstacles to the consideration of substantive change. Such change, it was agreed, was needed in order to respond to the critical fact that available resources could not continue to keep pace with the expansion of knowledge and its technologies and capital requirements or with the accelerating growth in the university's functions and programs. Easy as it was to recognize and assent to that proposition, it was very difficult to find any consensus on acceptable solutions, and the dynamic of growth moved inexorably on while the ambitions and expectations of a thriving academic culture remained basically unaltered.

Those were decades also of major controversies over affirmative action, over the educational value of diversity and the definition of such diversity, over the issues of political correctness and politicization in the university, and over the social responsibilities of universities in matters ranging from investment policy to the reform of public elementary and secondary education, from supporting economic development in local and regional communities to providing social services.

To read the literature on higher education over the past fifty years is to discover a litany of perpetual alarm and imminent catastrophe. The language of crisis was applied to many larger trends as well as to specific events or conditions: cyclical economic pressures; problems of the relation between universities and government and between universities and industry; diagnoses of educational failure and deeply polarized positions on the quality and direction of education and the relative priorities of teaching and research; arguments about whether the academy had become dangerously politicized; divergent views on multiculturalism, postmodernism, and other intellectual trends; divisions over the principles and policies that should guide broadened access to higher education; concerns about accountability; concerns over academic freedom. For some, the crisis of the university had to do with the prospects for supporting its ever more expensive ambitions for program and infrastructure; for others, with whether the university had lost its animating spirit, its intellectual and educational moorings. You will find the most distinguished and serious leaders of higher education and commentators on higher education in every decade asserting that *this* crisis is probably the most difficult ever.[3]

Today, of course, economic crisis has taken the forefront, and in a way that makes the impact of earlier downturns seem almost modest. It is useful to recall that the gloomiest forecasts of the late twentieth century have never quite been realized and that our very robust system of higher education has regularly survived the crises that in their times appeared so desperate. But that truth affords no clear lesson for the present and should certainly not encourage us to sit back and anticipate an ultimate return to the status quo ante. It is naturally tempting to take the option of muddling through, of dealing with immediate problems (which are certainly hard enough), and of making some adjustments at the margins while assuming that in general things will revert to their normal state.

But that will scarcely offer long-term health. In important ways the questions raised by current economic circumstances serve to expose and force us to confront longer-existing issues and deeper fault lines that have been building over the past decades. Ideally, responding to the pressures of today should mandate a serious assessment of and engagement in these issues with the goal of bringing about constructive choices and commitments designed to guide the defining goals of an institution. To pursue that strategy is to embark on a complex and difficult process that cannot of course produce sudden or comprehensive change but that can set a direction for the long term.

The questions being raised today have to do with whether universities can survive in their current form; whether the costs of education have mounted out of control; whether investment in higher education can be measured in terms of its outcomes and if so, whether the investment is worthwhile or properly targeted; whether university research is providing the social and economic benefits that are needed in the world; whether current programs of higher education are training students in the skills and forms of expertise required for the future. Unhappily, but not surprisingly, the emphasis in assessing the missions of higher education has shifted more acutely to higher education's responsibilities for professional and vocational training and further from the liberal arts, thus intensifying a trend that has long been with us.

Public perceptions of universities seem little affected by what universities say about themselves. Anyone will give you his or her conclusive views about what is wrong with higher education at the drop of a hat. This is in fact a subject on which everyone can be an expert, and that expertise is likely to focus less on the strengths than on the problems of our institutions and so to project a certain gloom.

As the tide of indignation over tuition costs continues to mount together with the demand for a better return (however that may be described) on the investment in education, we witness the difficulty of explaining, let alone justifying, their steady increase, as also of clarifying the nature and function of university endowments. It seems almost impossible to persuade people of the important difference between tuition list prices and the actual amount, after financial aid, that most students are required to pay, or of the relatively small percentage of most universities' budgets that depend on endowment. These matters of institutional wealth and cost command attention in the media every day, and they have come also to command a very visible position that will not soon fade on the congressional agenda in Washington.[4]

Discussions in the media tend to treat higher education as though it were a single entity rather than the mix of varied four-year public and private universities and colleges and two-year colleges that make up our system. Above all, it is common to identify higher education almost completely with collegiate education per se. The image of higher education is that of the undergraduate school, and most discussions of cost and quality and institutional policy have to do with the undergraduate experience. Accounts often treat research and graduate education as though they were forms of faculty self-indulgence that stand in the way of a sufficient commitment to undergraduate instruction and that spur the excesses of overspecialization. They perpetuate the widespread belief that teaching is subordinated to research, that faculty fail to take teaching seriously or do enough of it or do it effectively, that vocationalism and careerism have triumphed at the expense of liberal education—or (and this is equally if not more prevalent) that undergraduate education is too little concerned with "useful" learning of the sort that might bring social or professional benefit and prepare students for the "real" world.

Simultaneously the media bestow much positive attention on the achievements of university research while often expressing uneasiness about the ivory tower and urging universities to move toward greater outreach, to bring their expertise to bear more immediately on major national problems and engage more fully with their surrounding communities, thereby seeming to conceive the role of universities as that of suppliers of primarily applied research and agents of economic development, school reform, urban improvement, and other far-reaching social projects. The expectations for what universities can do (and, in these views, should be doing still more of) have climbed to ever greater heights even as the sense of constricted resources and excessive commitments overshadows their existence. The forces of consumerism, too, are on the rise, fueling new levels of expectation for the programs, services, and amenities that institutions should provide.

Some familiar stereotypes accompany much discussion of higher education: for example, the suspicion that tenure is just a kind of job security exempting its holders from having to work very hard, or that academic governance is designed as an obstruction to any real change in a complacent status quo, or that universities are wasteful, inefficient, badly managed organizations. The energetic lobbying of institutions of higher education and their Washington representatives (as well as of some professional disciplinary associations) and their eagerness in the pursuit of earmarks have reinforced a view of higher education as yet another special interest seeking self-interested political advantage while claiming to be thinking only higher thoughts. Indeed, higher education can be seen increasingly to conduct itself as though it were entitled to special privilege. At the same time, revelations of fraudulent conduct and of far-reaching conflicts of interest in academia have magnified doubts about the integrity and accountability of higher education and its capacity to make good on its claims to the disinterested pursuit of knowledge and effective self-regulation. In addition, the widespread belief that the campus is captive to political correctness has not waned while the conviction that a liberal or leftist conformity reigns at the expense of intellectual diversity has grown.

Such are some of the questions and attitudes that frame public perceptions and that affect the contemporary environment of higher education. It should be said, however, that public views of higher education reflect an ambivalence that has always surrounded this subject in our history. Side by side with the negative attitudes I have listed, there resides a very considerable faith in the power of higher education for the good and great pride in its institutions and accomplishments, coupled with a concern that American higher education remain, as it is so often said to be, the best in the world. The hyperbole and oversimplification that accompany so much rhetoric about the failings of higher education reveal also the strength of the desire to ensure the realization of that faith in practice.

Critiques of the state of higher education are not, of course, confined to the public world. Many of the most passionate attacks and most vigorous debates on the current shortcomings of our universities are, quite naturally, to be found in the academy itself.[5]

We can detect a special and intense disaffection in the mounting concern over what has come to be called the "commercialization" of universities. This central and troubling concern has spread both within and outside the academy. So, too, has anxiety over the "corporatization" of universities. (Such concerns have certainly existed in the past—think, for example, of both Veblen's and Hutchins's strictures—but today they have taken on new and still broader dimensions.) Occasionally the two terms are conflated; each is somewhat vaguely generalized and covers something of a range of issues. For many commentators, the phenomena of "commercialism" and "corporatization" represent a fundamental shift in the life of American higher education: namely, that it has come to be essentially market-driven rather than directed by an internal set of academic goals and values.

"Commercialism" is at one level assigned to the programs and practices of intercollegiate athletics, although these are scarcely new phenomena. At another level the term is aimed at the rather more complex issues arising from agreements forged between commercial entities and universities for the financial support of scientific research and development or of other projects in which a corporation will hope to benefit from applying the research or consulting assistance it receives in return. At yet another it may refer to the marketing techniques now employed by institutions of higher education in their quest for prestige and students. In the "corporate" realm, universities are seen as having sacrificed academic principles and priorities to the bottom line, to have become self-perpetuating bureaucratic organizations aping the features of corporate management, and to have been co-opted by an alien corporate culture. The heavy emphasis on fund-raising tasks for university leaders, the language of advertising, as in "branding" an institution, the expanded activity and the tone of public relations by which universities present themselves for purposes of recruitment, reputation, and visibility: all these feed into the allegation that universities have become "corporatized" and their leaders self-promoting "CEOs" rather than principled academic leaders. The role of the faculty in academic governance is asserted to have been seriously devalued and diminished in favor of a dominant corporate, top-down managerial culture.

In the background there exists a diffuse but pervasive sentiment in academic culture that tends to regard activities undertaken for money or priorities expressed in financial or managerial terms as probably suspect; it assumes that the corporate (or its stereotype) is inherently opposed to the academic spirit and that too much talk of such unattractive things as budgets and financial constraints verges on the "corporate"; higher values should prevail. The expressions "knowledge industry" or "higher education industry" act as red flags. The first phrase, nowadays so common, provoked savage reactions when noted in Kerr's book; it was held to demonstrate his contemptibly philistine idea of the university.[6]

In the instance of athletics, it seems to me that the questions go beyond the "commercial" to ones of skewed priorities, even in institutions that believe they have their priorities right while devoting disproportionate resources and admissions to recruiting athletic talent. The outrage so long voiced loudly and repeatedly over the scandals and excesses and practices of intercollegiate athletics has had very little effect. The reports and recommendations of countless commissions and task forces have seemed to encounter a nearly immovable object. In the meantime operating budgets for athletics have increased in recent years at more than double the rate of total spending for universities even as calls for serious reform have intensified. Here is a headline from the *Chronicle of Higher Education* introducing the latest report of the Knight Commission: "College Presidents Say They're Powerless to Control Big-Time Athletics."[7] Higher education has, to all intents and purposes, given up on this relentless problem, hoping perhaps that by a few NCAA reforms here and there, and some shaming of the most egregious from time to time, minor adjustments can make at least a little difference.

Another type of "commercialism" is more recent in origin and relates more directly to the central activities of the university, primarily, though not exclusively, those of scientific research. It has to do also with the larger issues that have long existed related to the strings and restrictions that accompany funds offered to universities, to what kinds of money they should appropriately accept, and above all to what conditions might be compatible with central academic values in forging alliances with any donor, whether government, corporation, or private individuals. The specific questions surrounding university-industry partnerships go immediately to the fear that the requirements of a for-profit corporation will be at odds with the academic code of free and open intellectual inquiry in teaching and research. The danger is always that financial ties could drive or distort the directions and processes of open research, of responsible teaching, and of the autonomy of the institution itself. For critics at one extreme, the rising number of alliances between researchers, their universities, and industry reflects a preoccupation on the part of universities with raising money at all costs, and by methods fraught with dangers to academic integrity and intellectual openness, with rewarding a style of entrepreneurship inconsistent with academic commitments, with giving precedence and privilege to the sciences, and with taking on corporate as opposed to academic values and so subordinating the goals of the university to the bottom line. The problems of conflicts of interest, not only for the institution, but also for the individual researcher (both as investigator and as teacher) are clearly immense, and these questions become still more acute in the case of spinoffs and of participation in the governance and profits of companies established on the foundation of an investigator's work.

On the other hand, when properly managed and when universities and their faculties have developed reasonably conservative policies relevant to the issues involved, clear benefits can come from partnerships between companies and investigators (think, for example, of translating basic findings into clinical therapies), and it makes no sense to assume that any such arrangements are inevitably tainted. Nor are they going to go away. There are those—here Derek Bok's careful discussion on the subject come to mind—who acknowledge the dangers of these associations and insist that they be approached very cautiously and selectively but who also see significant scientific, social, and intellectual value in such relationships and think it possible and realistic to define conditions central to the academic ethos and then legislate stringent guidelines for protecting the university's core values while enhancing resources for research in an environment of always limited federal and private funding. Here is a debate that within the academy raises different emphases in setting out the basic essence of the university and the balance that a research university should try to incorporate.[8]

Those same issues have long existed as concerns in the case of federal funding that might come with pressure to pursue priorities not necessarily the institution's own or with stipulations in conflict with the essential freedom that the university seeks to maintain. Today they obtain increasingly, too, in the case of individual donors whose gifts are intended to support specific agendas or interests of their own and who want to pursue those through the expertise of universities while keeping as much control as possible over the expenditure of their donated funds and the governance of their projects. In their enthusiasm for major gifts, universities can all too easily submit to choices in part decided for them and to direction outside the accepted forms of academic governance and, since restricted gifts are unlikely to cover the full costs of any program over time, find that they need to allocate discretionary funds for their support. That may well distort other options and goals. In the case of corporate relationships and faculty entrepreneurship, the problems of conflicts of interest and of loyalty, and both are serious and complex, add new but not insurmountable layers of difficulty.

Another form of "commercialism" in higher education these days has to do with the marketing of its institutions, with the kinds of strategies now being directed toward student recruitment and to elevating an institution's visibility and status. Cries of pain in a mounting crescendo issue from all who believe—and who can disagree?—that the appropriate marketplace for universities should be that of ideas, not products, and who consider that education and knowledge are being treated as commodities in a ceaseless race for students, resources, and recognition. It is instructive to observe universities participating in the ratings game set off by *U.S. News & World Report*'s annual rankings and to read about the various stratagems by which some attempt to influence the results. Despite the fashion of asserting a disdainful indifference toward such ratings, most institutions seem actually to pay them extraordinarily close attention and to claim that they have to take them seriously because prospective students and their families will do so. A large number of anecdotal accounts suggest that institutional behavior and cost can indeed be influenced by the desire to do well in the rankings. So, while everyone seems to agree that the whole basis for these rankings is seriously flawed, those who succeed in them won't fail to let you know how well they've done.[9]

The pronounced rise of consumerism in higher education has led its institutions to become increasingly responsive to their clients' expectations for programs, facilities, and services at ever more costly levels as they compete for students and try to satisfy the consumer mentality. Stories abound of luxurious dormitories and student centers, of grandiose arts and athletic centers, of ever expanded community service and internship programs, of space and counseling for every conceivable group or condition, of additional assistant deans and directors to preside over any function you might think of.

It is a truism that American higher education has benefited greatly from its pluralism of institutions, both public and private, and that the competition among them has been a key factor in the development and continuing vigor of our system of higher education. And so it has. But another side to this competition has become ever more evident, one that has the perverse effect of making institutions in some respects come to be more rather than less similar to one another and of thinking they *need* to be more alike in programs, facilities, and services if they are to compete in fact. Universities have moved in a more homogeneous direction, and in their turn colleges have in some respects become more like universities in their culture and aspirations. The competition to keep up with Jones University has stimulated an expensive contest—"arms race" is now the favored term here—for more of everything and the same of everything in the academic realm and beyond, whether in state-of-the-art facilities, new and improved student services, extracurricular opportunities, additional amenities of campus life, or other responses to consumer demand. It is interesting to find Laurence Veysey, in his history of the emergence of the American university, tracing such effects of what used generally to be thought in all respects a productive rivalry back to the 1890s and to a process of what he calls "blind imitation" that, in his view, encouraged not innovation but timidity and the attempt on the part of all universities to offer a "complete" course of study. "As American universities became more intensely competitive," he writes, "they became more standardized, less original, less fluid."[10]

It is a fact that the growth of nonacademic personnel over the past years has greatly outstripped that of faculty, and in the case of teaching appointments, the ranks of adjunct rather than tenure-track faculty have risen sharply. A recent study has concluded that support staff over the period 1987–2007 increased at almost double the rate of full-time equivalent instructional staff.[11] Administrative functions have multiplied, in part because of new obligations imposed on universities through law and regulation, in part to manage new programs, building construction and maintenance, and systems of information technology, as well as to manage a variety of ever more complex benefits and support services. Administration has a tendency to grow also because there is always more that *could* usefully be done or that is being demanded for some special, sometimes merely symbolic or even redundant, purpose.

Some portion of this growth has obviously to do with the greater attention devoted to student recruitment and services, public relations, and development, as well as with the creation of offices to handle expanded counseling of all kinds, study abroad, various kinds of community service, and deference to consumer desires. But at the same time, the growth of the nonfaculty population is in large measure tied directly to academic priorities and ventures that are usually faculty led. The proliferation of centers and institutes dedicated to research and policy studies is one striking example of this, the requirements of information technology another. The greater the research enterprise at any university, the larger its population of technicians, postdocs, and research associates. The broader its curricular and extracurricular range, the greater the need for technical and administrative support staff.

The assumptions of perpetual growth continue to dominate our universities. We must, of course, keep up with the growth of knowledge and developing methods of inquiry; we quite rightly want to keep strengthening the quality of the university's work in every area even as we are well aware that good ideas and high ambitions will inevitably outnumber the resources available at any given time even to the wealthiest institutions. The current economy has not created this condition, but it has thrown it into sharp relief and intensified the conflict between unlimited aspirations and limited resources, now exacerbated also by the prevailing forms of competition among universities.[12]

It is the nature, indeed the task, of universities to keep pace with always evolving areas of thought and discovery and to support promising risk-taking in research and education. The problem is not that of growth per se but that of selectivity, of identifying and building on the distinctive strengths of a given university and of defining and remaining faithful to those criteria of selection that will best serve its central academic priorities. All specific choices, as opposed to the guidelines for their assessment, can scarcely be planned in advance. It is essential to be open and responsive to unanticipated new directions and opportunities; a number will simply emerge out of the blue.

Nor does selectivity rest entirely in the university's own initiative. Some things simply cannot be afforded or supported; others present themselves opportunistically. The question of who does the selecting in our decentralized environment can be complex; that of locating authority for setting priorities even more so; that of concluding what to do without almost impossible. While collegial processes have always to be involved in making academic choices, extended consultation and endless study will often preempt clear decisions. "Careful consideration," runs an old saying, "is the best known defense against change." Our well-known reluctance even to consider doing without an existing program springs from a kind of senatorial courtesy or dread over confronting the hard politics of such deliberations as well as from the quite frequent and not unreasonable argument that academic fields necessarily relate to and reinforce one another so that to pull one thread is to unravel a much larger structure.[13]

In the end, however, trying to do all things or too many things will only result in weak or inadequately supported enterprises lacking in critical mass and quality. New programs generally come as additions, not replacements. Their costs in terms of additional people, space, and services are usually underestimated. The still more significant potential cost, which may be that doing this will mean there is something else one cannot do, is rarely weighed in sufficient depth, the pain of making hard trade-offs sidestepped. The most important consideration that should obtain in looking to the long term—namely, of what relation a project might have to the principal academic priorities and strengths of the university—may be deflected by immediate pressures to decide on a particular grant proposal or an attractive opportunity.

There are, then, many drivers of growth for universities, some theoretically very much under their control, others far less so. The underlying dynamic that universities cannot influence arises from the inherent character and accelerating pace of the investigation and learning for whose purposes they exist. That momentum, and its costs, can be observed at work in the sciences above all (but it is true not only of the sciences). Each stage of scientific discovery leads to a next that requires more resources, more capital outlays, more sophisticated technologies, more highly trained professionals. Each stage becomes more expensive, as do the state-of-the-art scientific education and training that follow and as do the requirements for infrastructure.[14] Universities have been assuming a higher proportion of the total costs of scientific research than they once did, and it is a real question whether they can sustain such continuing commitments across the whole spectrum of specializations they now support and whether those are already coming at the expense of other academic areas. As it is, there is anxiety over what is perceived as a widening distance between the sciences and other disciplines, those of the humanities in particular, and a prevalent fear that both resources and regard for the "softer" nonscientific fields are in decline.

In today's world of higher education an acute and pervasive sense of widening disparities between the more and less prosperous has grown. That the rich get richer, and even in hard times remain richer, and that the gap between the more and less well endowed can only increase, is an indisputable truth. At the same time, additional disparities of resources are appearing to loom large between public and private universities and to intensify among internal areas (schools, departments, programs) within the same institutions.[15]

Among nonscientists, and especially among humanists, there is the belief that universities are allocating ever greater priority and resources to the sciences and that the scientific enterprise may overwhelm the universities with an unsustainable level of need that can ultimately not be satisfied without large increases in revenues from external sources, which are in any case unlikely to keep pace, and that also raise the specter of fatally distorting academic values and skewing the appropriate balance of an academic community. Added to this is the fear that the ever heavier weight of academic medical centers, where they exist, and the shifting economies of medical education, research, and care already exercise, and may in the future impose still more, a disproportionate impact on the university as a whole.

Another critical element in the situation and outlook of the contemporary university and in the upward spiraling of costs is related to the changing role and costs of libraries and their technologies. The needs for investments in technology for purposes of education and scholarship are large movers in the equation and in the momentum of institutional growth. In addition, the broadly accepted goal of creating fuller access to higher education for people of all backgrounds and income levels, combined with rising tuition, the competition for students, and financial setbacks, will require still higher rates of financial aid and the need to fund and manage such major commitments. Thus in two areas of special significance for the future—the uses of technology to advance, strengthen, and support the many different areas of university activity and the long-term goal of fuller and more inclusive opportunities for people of all backgrounds (and thus also the society as a whole) to benefit from higher education—the trajectory of cost can only move higher. Whether hopes that the uses of technology in teaching and in administrative processes will ultimately help moderate expenditures is as yet, I think, still an open question.

Despite the very high quality (far greater than so many critics nowadays acknowledge) of much undergraduate instruction, the recognized prestige of such teaching in relation to research in the research universities has continued to decline, and it is not even wholly secure in the smaller colleges that pride themselves on being teaching institutions but that also demand research productivity from their faculties. More and more of the undergraduate teaching in universities is performed by part-time instructors not on the tenure track, while the formal class-time teaching requirements for regular faculty have been reduced, often unilaterally and at the expense of undergraduate courses.

I have the impression that the vigor of faculty participation or interest in general university affairs has atrophied somewhat as faculty live increasingly within their departments—and now also in the mounting number of semiautonomous institutes and centers that have become the coin of the academic realm. At the upper reaches of the academic profession, the styles of free agency and independent entrepreneurship have become ever more pronounced. But at the entry level opportunities have shriveled, and a long-awaited rebound in the academic marketplace has been delayed once again, now by the impact of economic recession.

Universities have increasingly come to be regarded as paternalistic welfare states whose citizens possess many entitlements. The campus as social community has resumed the role of acting in loco parentis for students who, although now in possession of personal freedoms once unimaginable, seem quite comfortable with that, so long as it is a *perfect* parent. The perfect parent is a generous and indulgent patron who does not set curfews or try to control children's lives but stands by to protect them from harm and punish their tormentors. As Peter Gomes has said, today's students "want to retain all their hard-won autonomy, while at the same time insisting that institutions assume a moral responsibility for protecting them from the consequences of their autonomy."[16]

We have seen how frequently over the past decades it has been alleged that universities have lost a once-flourishing intellectual community. These same times have witnessed the rise of a communitarian ideal that conceives the campus as ideally a model community in its social values and policies. The problems with this view are, I think, manifold. First, it values harmony and inoffensiveness, and thus a certain conformity, above the discomforts of contentiousness inherent in intellectual debate. Second, it dilutes and distracts from what should be the overriding imperatives of education and research by taking on tasks and activities that academic institutions are not primarily equipped or necessarily competent to perform. And third, it implies that the university as such is an agent of social change with a corporate role of advocacy in its relation to the social order.

Education should not be intended to make people comfortable; it is meant to make them think. Universities should be expected to provide the conditions within which hard thought, and therefore strong disagreement, independent judgment, and the questioning of stubborn assumptions, can flourish in an environment of the greatest freedom. They should of course encourage civility and discipline the truly unruly, but they should be very careful about what is appropriately subject to rule. The tendency to rule making, as in the case of speech codes designed to avoid unpleasantness and distress, elevates the model of the social community at the expense of the intellectual freedom central to a university's life.

Over their history, universities have been asked to enforce many different shades and kinds of conformity and different versions of what we now call "political correctness." Pressures of this sort have come not only from the outside; they are often internal ones as well. They can be explicit, as in the case of rules about speech, or more generally and subtly part of an accepted environment that fosters a certain form of orthodoxy or sense of limits or lives with the dominance of particular schools of thought. Those members of the academy, however well-meaning, who embrace such an environment in the name of some higher good will soon find weakened institutions of higher education and eroded conditions of academic freedom, both for the individual and for the university itself. It will be harder also to recognize and act on the principle that universities in their institutional capacity have the obligation to nurture and respect the differing individual convictions of each member.

Universities are special purpose institutions. Their work has to do with learning and teaching, the preservation and transmission of knowledge, the search for new knowledge, and the interpretation or reinterpretation of what has over the centuries been created, experienced, and thought. Universities, uniquely among the institutions of our world, look in their work to the long term. Theirs is a "culture of criticism" that will always be seen by some as threatening or seriously unsettling in the immediate term. The specific role of universities requires institutional conditions of corporate autonomy. It requires the institution to sustain an environment open to rigorous and searching debate and to the expression of independent, often unpopular, points of view. It requires universities to enable the individual freedom of the faculty member in his or her professional capacity, and acting in accordance with professional criteria of scientific and scholarly integrity, to be free from external or internal pressures in the activities of teaching, research, writing, speaking, or participation in university affairs and governance, and free to be judged by academic standards in matters of appointment and promotion and retention (reinforced by the institution of tenure). Academic freedom, as Matthew W. Finkin and Robert C. Post have recently written, "establishes the liberty necessary to advance knowledge, which is the liberty to practice the scholarly profession." And again: "Academic freedom is not the freedom to speak or to teach just as one wishes. It is the freedom to pursue the scholarly profession, inside and outside the classroom, according to the norms and standards of that profession."[17] In short, academic freedom is situated in the specific vocation of the scholar and teacher; it defines the freedoms required to pursue that vocation and to do so within the framework of the intellectual and professional responsibilities that pursuit assumes.

Of course no university can be fully autonomous. For the public universities, the relation to their state governments, and for all research universities, their relation to the federal government and potential indebtedness to others with some power of the purse, must suggest at least some limitations and at most an unhealthy dependence. At the level of the individual faculty member, there have occurred dramatic instances of exposure to hostile political forces and of weak response on the part of many universities, as in the times of McCarthyism, of the Cold War at its height and indeed at times of war more generally. Less visible is the multitude of pressures from many directions—alumni, legislators, donors, administrators, special interest groups of all sorts, even colleagues—that may in some way constrain the full exercise of intellectual liberty. Frontal assaults are in some ways easier to counteract; far more complicated is the range of issues inherent in the gradually erosive effects made possible by the environment of universities today, both external and internal. The issues posed to freedom of inquiry by the commercial ties developed by universities or individual faculty members represent just one example of a complex challenge of this sort. In considering the central questions of academic freedom, "the issue," writes Craig Calhoun, is not just whether free speech is repressed, important and basic as that is, or whether individuals suffer in their careers for expressing controversial views. It is whether and how universities bring knowledge, diverse perspectives, and competing analyses into the public sphere. Doing this may well depend on freedom from censorship and repression, but it also depends on a variety of intellectual choices and institutional conditions. The defense of academic freedom needs to be based on the effectiveness of academia itself in capitalizing on freedom and other conditions to deliver knowledge as a public good.[18]

"Academic freedom" is too often invoked quite carelessly, as though any strong criticism of or extreme attack on views advocated by members of the academic community could be interpreted as an assault on academic freedom or the indicator of a new "McCarthyism." Those distortions diminish the central core of what we should understand by academic freedom, appearing to defend claims of privilege and sanctuary rather than to affirm the nexus of rights and responsibilities and of institutional conditions that academic freedom entails, and ultimately make its defense more difficult when the threat is real or could become so.

The issue of preserving academic freedom for institution and individual alike is closely tied to that of taking institutional positions on social and political matters. Clearly universities can and should speak out on questions that, when they become questions also of public policy, go directly to their essential purposes and conditions. These may include (and indeed have included) a variety of issues related to admissions policies, appointments procedures, research funding and regulation, financial aid, and, most important, the sustenance of academic freedom for their members; in short, those areas over which the greatest possible control is needed for universities in pursuit of their special missions. Of course there may be considerable disagreement over the particulars of such questions within a given institution, but there is broad agreement that public advocacy on behalf of the university's closest interests as an educational entity is appropriate. The difficult problems arise when the university is asked to adopt policies or to take positions in order to give voice and authority to the views of a group advocating that the university declare itself and act as a moral force engaged with the larger world in matters of urgency. In these cases, the questions do not emerge from the special function of universities; they are ones for all citizens and ones on which individuals, in their capacity as citizens, will disagree. Universities do have the responsibility to provide a space of openness and freedom in which those disagreements can be examined and argued and matters of public policy analyzed and discussed, but to take an institutional position on such questions would imply a claim to speak on behalf of all its members in matters of political and social consequence. To accept that claim would be to lessen the freedom of the university community's individual members as well as to assert a role for the university that would soon erode its autonomy.

It is of course one thing to set guidelines on this subject, quite another to determine precisely when and how they are to be applied in exceptional circumstances. As the Kalven Report, issued at the University of Chicago in 1967, put it, there will in rare cases be corporate activities of the university that "may appear so incompatible with paramount social values as to require careful assessment of the consequences."[19] It is here, over the question of what is truly the rare case, that the most intense battles have been fought over the past several decades, usually over universities' investment and other business-related activities (and often in effect rearguing the presumption that the university should not declare political positions or undertake political action).

Such debates remind us of the recurrent need to reflect on the nature of the research university, to consider its potential strengths and to acknowledge also the limitations these impose on trying to transform it into a social utopia rather than fortifying and extending its unique purposes of education, scholarly learning, and the preservation and creation of knowledge within the conditions of the greatest possible freedom. And those purposes, I think, are surely utopian enough.

Conclusion

In cataloging the elements (including those of public perception) that seem to me most prominent, and most deep-seated, in the world of universities today, I have probably sounded a note more negative than I intend. For I think the state of our universities in general remains very strong and that the tendency to see all imperfections or problems as inevitably fatal is absurdly excessive. It is obvious, too, that for all the obstacles in the way of legislating or accepting major change, universities have in fact developed greatly and adapted creatively, if not always with a systematic plan and certainly not simply on their own, to the exigencies and opportunities of changing times.

But I think also that we would do well to return to basics, to our academic center, and to ask ourselves what, in the end, is the essential work of a university and how we can best guide ourselves by that purpose in a complex academic universe of many interests and roles. In doing so, we need to avoid the temptations of easy nostalgia and begin from where we are, in a universe of highly complicated multipurpose universities, in a world of rapidly advancing knowledge and technological innovation and globalization, in an environment of tensions over educational access and its goals and higher learning and its costs, and in an academic context accustomed to a long time horizon to work through the processes of collegial discussion.

It seems clear that universities need to confront some painful realities and become more deliberately selective in what they choose to do. Universities are overstretched in their range of programs, overbuilt in physical facilities, and overburdened by an excess of ambitions, expectations, and demands. The competition among them has led to greater homogeneity rather than a constructive diversity of institutional profiles and of distinctive individual excellence. We would be better off if it were possible to assert more clearly chosen aims and realize those in depth, to build on each institution's comparative strengths, to adopt more modest (which is not to say shabby) styles of life, and, above all, to remember that our mission is not to change the world, even if we could, but to advance and preserve knowledge and to educate those who may indeed help change it, tasks that are quite sufficiently world-changing in themselves. To say that we should be more modest and more realistic in what we profess to do is not to diminish the university's unique value to the social order, nor does it mean that universities should abandon all public service. But the forms of service they undertake or sanction should proceed from their educational and scholarly purposes, from what they do best or from what they can do that other institutions cannot do or do as well. The insistent demands for universities to make a difference in every important good cause that merits attention will only divert them endlessly from the central contributions that are theirs specifically to make. So, too, does the idea that the university's ultimate goal is to exemplify social virtue.[1]

Greater differentiation among institutions might encourage each to focus on its own particular mix of academic priorities and responsibilities and give greater definition to that community's shared commitments. It might give some illumination to prospective students' decisions as to where to apply, either to college (but this is hard at the age of seventeen) or to graduate school. It would certainly not stifle competition and might even help redirect competition into channels more removed from an arms race. At the same time, there will be significant opportunities found in expanding collaborations among institutions, for example, in joint ventures related to major areas of science that require costly space and instrumentation, in library networks, in sharing facilities for the arts, in joint programs such as teaching rare languages or developing newer fields or subfields as additions to the curriculum. We still have far to go in exploring the most effective possibilities for collaboration now afforded by technology.

We academics are generally better at the critical diagnosis of other institutions than of our own and more inclined to urge recommendations for change on others than on ourselves. We are professionally skilled at analyzing the potential drawbacks and negative outcomes implicit in almost any course of action; it is our business to discern the macrocosm in the microcosm and to know that taking an inch will all too likely mean taking a mile. As someone has remarked, "The trouble with intellectuals is that they can think of something with respect to anything." We are suspicious of administrative authority and hostile to bureaucracy, and we are likely to wonder about the motives behind the questions they ask us to consider. We take collegiality seriously and the claims of individual opinion and each colleague's right to dissent still more so. All these characteristics complicate the work we have to do, without justifying its evasion.

The history of universities is not one of uninterrupted progress, and the great successes achieved by the postwar universities in their turn created problems yet to be addressed. It will take a good dose of realism and an unfaltering commitment to academic imperatives to assess and to rebalance the elements of what I call the "stripped down university." But that is where we need to start. It would be foolish to suggest that universities can simply do this on their own or that they could or should turn back their clocks to some earlier time, naive to imagine that their course can be considered in isolation from the complex social and political contexts in which they are embedded. But when all is said and done, it is remarkable how resilient our world of higher education has been and how great are the opportunities, in yet another time of crisis and if we can summon the initiative, to strengthen its promise for the future.

NOTES

INTRODUCTION

1. Two recent books on higher education illustrate the continuing preoccupation with these two ways of thinking about the university. Jonathan Cole's *The Great American University: Its Rise to Preeminence, Its Indispensable National Role, Why It Must Be Protected* (New York: Public Affairs, 2009) provides a ringing defense of the research university based on its contributions to the creation of new knowledge and the social benefits of university research. The polemics of Andrew Hacker and Claudia Dreifus in *Higher Education? How Colleges Are Wasting Our Money and Failing Our Kids—And What We Can Do about It* (New York: Times Books, 2010) are directed against what they see as the research orientation of universities, a failure to put teaching undergraduates first, and the degradation of education in the liberal arts.

2. Clark Kerr, *The Uses of the University*, 5th ed. (Cambridge, MA: Harvard University Press, 2001), 113.

1. *THE USES OF THE UNIVERSITY* REVISITED

1. Clark Kerr, *The Uses of the University*, 5th ed. (Cambridge, MA: Harvard University Press, 2001), 159–60.

2. Mary Ann Dzuback, *Robert M. Hutchins: Portrait of an Educator* (Chicago: University of Chicago Press, 1991), 203.

3. Robert Maynard Hutchins, *The Higher Learning in America,* 2nd ed. (New Haven, CT: Yale University Press, 1962), 52.

4. Ibid., 94, 95. Emphasis added.

5. Ibid., 96, 99.

6. Ibid., 105.

7. Robert Maynard Hutchins, *Education for Freedom* (Baton Rouge: Louisiana State University Press, 1943), 98.

8. Ibid., 100.

9. Hutchins, *Higher Learning,* 66.

10. Hutchins, *Education for Freedom,* 25, 26.

11. Hutchins, Trustee-Faculty Dinner Speech, January 12, 1944 (Robert Hutchins Papers, Box 26, Folder 3, University of Chicago Library).

12. A.J. Liebling, *Chicago: The Second City* (New York: Knopf, 1952), 100.

13. Hutchins, Confidential Memo (to the Board of Trustees), July 2, 1942, 9.

14. Hutchins, Trustee-Faculty Dinner Speech, 8.

15. Discussions of these events, and of Hutchins's view of presidential authority and his relations with the faculty, can be found in Dzuback, *Robert M. Hutchins,* chap. 9; William H. McNeill, *Hutchins' University* (Chicago: University of Chicago Press, 1991), chap. 5; Harry S. Ashmore, *Unseasonable Truths: The Life of Robert Maynard Hutchins* (Boston: Little, Brown, 1989), 237–43; Milton Mayer, *Robert Maynard Hutchins: A Memoir* (Berkeley: University of California Press, 1993), chaps. 31–34.

16. On Hutchins's political views and ambitions, and on his anti-interventionist position before World War II, see especially Ashmore, *Unseasonable Truths;* and Mayer, *Robert Maynard Hutchins.* See also John W. Boyer, *The University of Chicago and War in the Twentieth Century,* Occasional Papers on Higher Education, no. 11 (Chicago: College of the University of Chicago, 2003), 64–69.

17. Kerr, *Uses of the University,* 25.

18. Robert Maynard Hutchins, *The University of Utopia* (Chicago: University of Chicago Press, 1953), 87. See also Robert Maynard Hutchins, "The Freedom of the University," *Ethics* 61 (1951): 95–104; and "The Meaning and Significance of Academic Freedom," *Annals of the American Academy of Political and Social Science* 300 (1955): 72–78. On the Walgreen and Broyles Commission cases and on Hutchins's anti-McCarthy statements, see the biographies cited above, as well as John W. Boyer, *Academic Freedom and the Modern University: The Experience of the University of Chicago,* Occasional Papers on Higher Education (Chicago: College of the University of Chicago, 2002), 23–84; and Geoffrey Stone, *Perilous Times: Free Speech in Wartime from the Sedition Act of 1798 to the War on Terrorism* (New York: Norton, 2004), chap. 5.

19. Kerr, *Uses of the University,* 113.

20. Ibid., 154–55.

21. Ibid., 196.

22. Ibid., 43.

23. Clark Kerr, *The Gold and the Blue,* vol. 1 (Berkeley: University of California Press, 2001), pt. 4.

24. Kerr, *Uses of the University,* 71.

25. Ibid., 99.

26. See Kerr, *Uses of the University,* 22.

27. Quoted in Richard Storr, *Harper's University: The Beginnings* (Chicago: University of Chicago Press, 1966), 103.

2. THE UNIVERSITY IDEA AND LIBERAL LEARNING

1. The general prevalence of such announced goals is nicely pointed out by Charles T. Clotfelter, *Buying the Best: Cost Escalation in Elite Higher Education* (Princeton, NJ: Princeton University Press, 1996), 23–24.

2. On the medieval universities, see especially H. De Ridder-Symoens, ed., *A History of the University in Europe,* vol. 1, *Universities in the Middle Ages* (Cambridge: Cambridge University Press, 1992); Charles

Homer Haskins, *The Renaissance of the Twelfth Century* (Cambridge, MA: Harvard University Press, 1927); and Olaf Pedersen, *The First Universities: Studium generale and the Origins of University Education in Europe* (Cambridge: Cambridge University Press, 1997).

3. On the liberal arts in the medieval universities, see Gordon Leff, "The Trivium and the Three Philosophies," and Jacques Verger, "Patterns," in De Ridder-Symoens, *History of the University in Europe*, 1:307–36 and 1:41–45, respectively; and Pedersen, *The First Universities*, 271–300. On the longer history of the liberal arts and their definitions and their roles in the university curriculum, see especially Bruce A. Kimball, *Orators and Philosophers: A History of the Idea of Liberal Education* (New York: Teachers College, Columbia University, 1986); and Francis Oakley, *Community of Learning: The American College and the Liberal Arts Tradition* (New York: Oxford University Press, 1992).

4. Thomas More, *Selected Letters,* ed. Elizabeth F. Rogers (New Haven, CT: Yale University Press, 1961), 96, 101–2. The discussion of *Utopia* is based on book 2 of the text. There is of course an enormous bibliography on Renaissance humanism as well as on More; I have offered my own—not greatly controversial—interpretations here. For the early modern period and for the place of the liberal arts in the universities of the sixteenth century and after, see H. De Ridder-Symoens, ed., *A History of the University in Europe,* vol. 2: *Universities in Early Modern Europe (1500–1800)* (Cambridge: Cambridge University Press, 1996), esp. chaps. 1 (Walter Ruegg), 11 (Olaf Pedersen), and 14 (Laurence Brockliss).

5. John Henry Newman, *The Idea of a University,* ed. Frank M. Turner (New Haven, CT: Yale University Press, 1996). See Sheldon Rothblatt, "The Idea of the Idea of a University and Its Antithesis," in Rothblatt, *The Modern University and Its Discontents: The Fate of Newman's Legacies in Britain and America* (Cambridge: Cambridge University Press, 1997), 7: "It was Newman who transformed the inherited legalistic description of a university as a corporate body possessing endowments and privileges pertaining to learning into a thrilling emotion-laden, higher order conception of education."

6. See Frank M. Turner, "Newman's University and Ours," in Newman, *Idea of a University,* 282–301. Jaroslav Pelikan's *The Idea of a University: A Reexamination* (New Haven, CT: Yale University Press, 1992) offers a direct reflection on and adaptation of Newman to the modern university as Pelikan conceives it.

7. Newman, *Idea of a University,* 78–79, 89–90, 98, 99, 109, 125–26.

8. See Turner, "Newman's University and Ours," 284.

9. See Newman, *Idea of a University,* 125–26.

10. See Lenore O'Boyle, "Learning for Its Own Sake: The German University as Nineteenth-Century Model," *Comparative Studies in Society and History* 25, no. 1 (January 1983): 3–25; Charles McClelland, *State, Society and University in Germany: 1700–1914* (Cambridge: Cambridge University Press, 1980), esp. 101–89.

11. On the general history of American higher education, see especially Roger A. Geiger, *To Advance Knowledge: The Growth of the American Research Universities, 1900–1940* (New York: Oxford University Press, 1986), and *Research and Relevant Knowledge: American Research Universities since World War II* (New York: Oxford University Press, 1993); Julie A. Reuben, *The Making of the Modern University: Intellectual Transformation and the Marginalization of Morality* (Chicago: University of Chicago Press, 1996); Frederick Rudolph, *The American College and University: A History,* 2nd ed. (Athens: University of Georgia Press, 1990), and *Curriculum: A History of the American Undergraduate Course of Study since 1636* (San Francisco: Jossey-Bass, 1977); John R. Thelin, *A History of American Higher Education* (Baltimore, MD: Johns Hopkins University Press, 2004); Laurence R. Veysey, *The Emergence of the American University* (Chicago: University of Chicago Press, 1965).

12. Here again, there is of course a very large bibliography. Both Kimball, *Orators and Philosophers,* and Oakley, *Community of Learning* (esp. chap. 2) offer clear overviews, histories, and definitions of these two broad understandings of the liberal arts.

13. Henry P. Tappan, "University Education," in *American Higher Education: A Documentary History,* vol. 2, ed. Richard Hofstadter and Wilson Smith (Chicago: University of Chicago Press, 1961), 488–511.

14. Eliot in 1908, as quoted in Samuel Eliot Morison, *Three Centuries of Harvard* (Cambridge, MA: Harvard University Press, 1936), 335–36. On Eliot, the elective principle, and its consequences, see Rudolph, *The American College and University*, chap. 14; Hugh Hawkins, *Between Harvard and America: The Educational Leadership of Charles W. Eliot* (New York: Oxford University Press, 1972); W. B. Carnochan, *The Battle of the Curriculum* (Stanford, CA: Stanford University Press, 1993), 9–18.

15. Oscar Handlin, quoted in *Glimpses of the Harvard Past* (Cambridge, MA: Harvard University Press, 1986), 109.

16. William Rainey Harper, unpublished report of 1892 excerpted in Thomas Wakefield Goodspeed, *A History of the University of Chicago: The First Quarter Century* (Chicago: University of Chicago Press, 1916), 145–46. For the founding and early years of the University of Chicago, see also Richard J. Storr, *Harper's University: The Beginnings* (Chicago: University of Chicago Press, 1966).

17. William Rainey Harper, "The Quinquennial Statement of the President," *University Record* 1, no. 16 (July 17, 1896): 254.

18. Woodrow Wilson, "Princeton in the Nation's Service," in *College and State: Educational, Literary, and Political Papers (1875–1913)*, vol. 1, ed. Ray Stannard Baker and William E. Dodd (New York: Harper, 1925), 259–85, esp. 263–84; quotations on 263–64.

19. Useful summaries of these views (themselves existing along a considerable spectrum) can be found in Reuben, *The Making of the Modern University*, 211–29; and Carnochan, *Battle of the Curriculum*, 39–67.

20. Thorstein Veblen, *The Higher Learning in America: A Memorandum on the Conduct of Universities by Business Men*, excerpted in Hofstadter and Smith, *American Higher Education*, 2:818–32.

21. *General Education in a Free Society* (Cambridge, MA: Harvard University Press, 1945), 43, 46–47. For some discussions of the history, different styles, and fortunes of general education, see Christopher Jencks and David Riesman, *The Academic Revolution*, 2nd ed. (Chicago: University of Chicago Press, 1969), 492–504; Daniel Bell, *The Reforming of General Education: The Columbia College Experience in Its National Setting* (New York: Columbia University Press, 1966); F. Champion Ward,

ed., *The Idea and Practice of General Education: An Account of the College of the University of Chicago* (Chicago: University of Chicago Press, 1950); Oakley, *Community of Learning*, 63–64, 122–27; Carnochan, *Battle of the Curriculum*, 88–99; John W. Boyer, *A Twentieth-Century Cosmos: The New Plan and the Origins of General Education at Chicago*, Occasional Papers on Higher Education 16 (Chicago: College of the University of Chicago, 2007); Louis Menand, *The Marketplace of Ideas: Reform and Resistance in the American University* (New York: Norton, 2010), 23–57. Two recent reports on general education, both issued in 2007, are Harvard's *Report of the Task Force on General Education*, www.fas.harvard.edu/secfas/General_Education_Final_Report.pdf; and *General Education in the 21st Century: A Report of the University of California Commission on General Education in the 21st Century* (Berkeley: Center for Studies in Higher Education, University of California, Berkeley, 2007). On the decline of general education, see Andrew Delbanco, "The Endangered University," *New York Review of Books* 52 (March 24, 2005): 19–22. Delbanco quotes Arnold Rampersad saying that "the Core is like the interstate highway system: we are glad we have it, but we could never build it today" (19).

22. These debates have taken place over several decades and involve a very large literature, from academic to popular and from apoplectic to thoughtful. Allan Bloom's *The Closing of the American Mind: How Higher Education Has Failed Democracy and Impoverished the Souls of Today's Students* (New York: Simon & Schuster, 1987) was perhaps the principal book, selling surprisingly well, that served to intensify public debate; it was followed by a spate of others, of which Roger Kimball's *Tenured Radicals: How Politics Has Corrupted Our Higher Education* (New York: Harper Perennial, 1990) is perhaps most significant. Oakley, in his *Community of Learning*, surveys much of the literature published before 1992 and brings a balanced thoughtfulness to its analysis and discussion. John R. Searle's essays, "The Storm over the University," *New York Review of Books* 37, no. 19 (December 6, 1990): 34–42; and "Is There a Crisis in American Higher Education?" *Bulletin of the American Academy of Arts and Sciences* 46 (January 1993): 24–47, stand out for their serious examination of both sides of the basic disputes and their complexities

and for his careful conclusions. The volume edited by Paul Berman, *Debating P.C.: The Controversy over Political Correctness on College Campuses* (New York: Dell, 1992), offers a good selection of writings on opposing sides.

23. Searle, "Is There a Crisis in Higher Education?," 30: "I do not know any intellectual tradition that is as savagely self-critical as the Western tradition." On the point of the assertedly "political" character of the curriculum, he writes: "Another fallacious move made by the challengers is to infer from the fact that the university's educational efforts invariably have political consequences that therefore the primary objective of the university, and the primary criteria for assessing its success or failure, should be political. The conclusion does not follow from the premise. Obviously, everything has political consequences. . . . In this sense everything is political" (39).

24. Irving Howe, "The Value of the Canon," in Berman, *Debating P.C.*, 159, 162.

25. "The American College Teacher: National Norms for 2007–2008" (Higher Education Research Institute at UCLA, March 2009), discussed by institute director Sylvia Hurtado in the *Chronicle of Higher Education,* March 5, 2009.

26. Jaroslav Pelikan, *Scholarship and Its Survival* (n.p.: Carnegie Foundation for the Advancement of Teaching, 1983), 26.

3. USES (AND MISUSES)
OF THE UNIVERSITY TODAY

1. Allan Bloom, *The Closing of the American Mind: How Higher Education Has Failed Democracy and Impoverished the Souls of Today's Students* (New York: Simon & Schuster, 1987). Francis Oakley, in *Community of Learning: The American College and the Liberal Arts Tradition* (New York: Oxford University Press, 1992), 127 et seq., quite rightly argues that the impact of the sixties was greatly exaggerated by the critics of higher education and of the newer intellectual fashions of the seventies and eighties; the point here, however, is that those critics believed that the sixties

were responsible for the evils that followed and helped others believe it as well.

2. For the rise of the postwar university in a period that saw the decisive connection forged between federal funding and university research in a time of growth and prosperity, see Roger L. Geiger, *Research and Relevant Knowledge: American Research Universities since World War II* (New York: Oxford University Press, 1993); Hugh Davis Graham and Nancy Diamond, *The Rise of American Research Universities: Elites and Challengers in the Postwar Era* (Baltimore, MD: Johns Hopkins University Press, 1997); and the summaries offered in Donald Kennedy, *Academic Duty* (Cambridge, MA: Harvard University Press, 1997), and Frank H. T. Rhodes, *The Creation of the Future: The Role of the American University* (Ithaca, NY: Cornell University Press, 2001). On the "golden age" as an anomaly, see Donald Kennedy, "Making Choices in the Research University," *Daedalus* 122, no. 4 (Fall 1993): 132; Kennedy, *Academic Duty*, 45, 151; and William G. Bowen, commenting in *Minerva* 30 (1992): 175: "it seems clearer and clearer that that decade was an aberration in almost every respect."

3. John R. Searle's words of 1990 remain relevant. In "The Storm over the University" (*New York Review of Books* 37, no. 19 [December 6, 1990]: 34–42), he wrote, "I cannot recall a time when American education was not in a 'crisis.' We have lived through Sputnik (when we were 'falling behind the Russians'), through the era of 'Johnny can't read,' and through the upheavals of the Sixties. Now a good many books are telling us that the university is going to hell in several different directions at once. . . . As with taxation and relations between the sexes, higher education is essentially and continuously contested territory" (34). Later, in "Is There a Crisis in Higher Education?" (*Bulletin of the American Academy of Arts and Sciences* 46 [January 1993]: 24–47), Searle went on to describe his sense of a decline in higher education, above all in its intellectual and educational moorings. Others have pointed to unprecedented challenges of demography, technology, and governance. The repeated rhetoric of crisis over the past decades has also, of course, been strongly focused on resource issues, with the condition of

the economy, the vagaries of federal funding (above all for science), and accompanying problems in the universities' relationship with government, with the political process, and with fears of a fall in public trust. By way of example, one has only to read the articles in the fall 1993 (vol. 122) issue of *Daedalus* devoted to the American research university or the collection of essays edited by Steven Brint in *The Future of the City of Intellect: The Changing American University* (Stanford, CA: Stanford University Press, 2002), or the recent book by Robert Zemsky, *Making Reform Work: The Case for Transforming American Higher Education* (New Brunswick, NJ: Rutgers University Press, 2009).

4. Excellent treatments of the cost structures and drivers of costs for research universities are found in Robert B. Archibald and David H. Feldman, *Why Does College Cost So Much?* (Oxford: Oxford University Press, 2010); Charles T. Clotfelter, *Buying the Best: Cost Escalation in Elite Higher Education* (Princeton, NJ: Princeton University Press, 1996); Ronald L. Ehrenberg, *Tuition Rising* (Cambridge, MA: Harvard University Press, 2002); Roger L. Geiger, *Knowledge and Money: Research Universities and the Paradox of the Marketplace* (Stanford, CA: Stanford University Press, 2004); and Burton A. Weisbrod, Jeffrey Ballou, and Evelyn D. Asch, *Mission and Money: Understanding the University* (Cambridge: Cambridge University Press, 2009). The still increasing volume of media articles and columns that ignore such studies and view universities as hoarding large endowments, maintaining expensive programs, supporting a less than fully productive faculty, and adding luxurious buildings and amenities, while ratcheting up tuition costs to unsupportable levels, are well represented in Peter Coy, "Academic Endowments: The Curse of Hoarded Treasure," *Business Week,* March 1, 2009; Eric Gibson, "Pleading Poverty: Colleges Want Parents to Foot the Bill for Their Largess," *Wall Street Journal,* December 5, 2008; Ron Lieber, "Why College Costs Rise, Even in a Recession," *New York Times,* September 5, 2009.

5. A sampling (quite selective) of recent books by professors alarmed by what they see as the commercialization and corporatization of the university, by an increasing utilitarianism and materialism

opposed to broader educational values, and/or by the decline of the humanities in particular, includes Bill Readings, *The University in Ruins* (Cambridge, MA: Harvard University Press, 1996); Alvin B. Kernan, ed., *What's Happened to the Humanities?* (Princeton, NJ: Princeton University Press, 1997); David L. Kirp, *Shakespeare, Einstein, and the Bottom Line: The Marketing of Higher Education* (Cambridge, MA: Harvard University Press, 2003); James Engell and Anthony Dangerfield, *Saving Higher Education in the Age of Money* (Charlottesville: University of Virginia Press, 2005); Jennifer Washburn, *University, Inc: The Corporate Corruption of American Higher Education* (New York: Basic Books, 2005); Anthony T. Kronman, *Education's End: Why Our Colleges and Universities Have Given Up on the Meaning of Life* (New Haven, CT: Yale University Press, 2009); and Gayle Tuchman, *Wannabe U: Inside the Corporate University* (Chicago: University of Chicago Press, 2009). In addition, see the essays by Andrew Delbanco in the *New York Review of Books:* "Colleges: An Endangered Species?" (52 [March 10, 2005]: 1), "The Endangered University" (52 [March 24, 2005]: 19–22), and "The Universities in Trouble" (56 [May 14, 2009]).

6. See John H. Schaar and Sheldon S. Wolin, "Berkeley and the Fate of the Multiversity," *New York Review of Books* 4 (March 11, 1965); and Kerr's response, ibid., April 8, 1965.

7. Libby Sanders, "College Presidents Say They're Powerless to Control Big-Time Athletics," *Chronicle of Higher Education,* October 26, 2009. On intercollegiate athletics and their commercialization, see Derek Bok, *Universities in the Marketplace: The Commercialization of Higher Education* (Princeton, NJ: Princeton University Press, 2003), chap. 3. On the growth of universities' expenditures on athletics, see Libby Sanders, "Sports Budgets Outpace Spending over All," *Chronicle of Higher Education,* May 1, 2009; and Doug Lederman's article in *Inside Higher Education,* January 19, 2010. On skepticism concerning reform, see Katie Thomas, "Call to Curb Athletic Spending Strikes Some as Unrealistic," *Chronicle of Higher Education,* October 27, 2009; and David Moltz, "Powerless, or Passing the Buck?," *Inside Higher Education,* October 27, 2009.

8. On the issues of university-industry partnerships, faculty entre-preneurship, and the concerns over commercialization of research and its implications, see in particular the thorough and balanced assess-ment by Derek Bok, *Universities in the Marketplace,* esp. chap. 6 and 11–20, 77–78, 115 and n. 4, 118–21; and the variety of perspectives presented in Hans Radder, *The Commodification of Academic Research* (Pittsburgh, PA: University of Pittsburgh Press, 2010). For a more vigorous defense (accompanied by clear guidelines to guard against potential distor-tions of academic norms), see Rhodes, *The Creation of the Future,* chap. 9; Charles M. Vest, *The American Research University from World War II to World Wide Web* (Berkeley: University of California Press, 2007); and Jonathan R. Cole, *The Great American University: Its Rise to Preeminence, Its Indispensable National Role, Why It Must Be Protected* (New York: Public Affairs, 2009). For a more negative view (two of many), see Kirp, *Shakespeare, Einstein, and the Bottom Line;* and Washburn, *University, Inc.* Cf. Zemsky, *Making Reform Work;* Richard Chait, "*The Academic Revolution Revisited,*" in Brint, *The Future of the City of Intellect,* 293–321; Geiger, *Knowledge and Money;* and Ellen Schrecker, *The Lost Soul of American Higher Education: Corporatization, the Assault on Academic Freedom, and the End of the American University* (New York: New Press, 2010).

9. See "Using the Rankings," *Inside Higher Education,* December 6, 2010. See also Eric Kelderman, "Law-School Cost Is Pushed Up by Quest for Prestige, not Accreditation, GAO Survey Finds," *Chronicle of Higher Education,* October 26, 2009, citing a reluctance on the part of law schools to admit minority applicants with lower LSAT scores "because the median LSAT score is a key factor in the *U.S. News & World Report* rankings." On the rankings, see also Zemsky, *Making Reform Work,* 72–89.

10. On one analysis of the "arms race," see Gordon C. Winston, "The Positional Arms Race in Higher Education," Discussion Paper No. 54, Williams Project on the Economics of Higher Education, April 2000. Another area of competition can be found in the continuing push to promote the "selectivity" and excellence of their student bod-ies on the part of colleges and universities by stimulating the volume

of applications received from year to year. A thoughtful article on this subject is Eric Hoover, "Application Inflation: When Is Enough Enough?," *New York Times,* November 5, 2010. See also Laurence R. Veysey, *The Emergence of the American University* (Chicago: University of Chicago Press, 1965), 330–31.

11. Daniel Bennett, *Trends in the Higher Education Labor Force: Identifying Changes in Worker Composition and Productivity,* A Report from the Center for College Affordability and Productivity, Washington, DC, April 2009. For a critical commentary arguing that such trends need to be analyzed from a larger perspective and that they are actually similar to those in the for-profit world, see Robert B. Archibald and David H. Feldman, "College Administrations Are Too Bloated? Compared with What?," *Chronicle of Higher Education,* August 10, 2009.

12. On the insatiable appetite for more that is inherent in the lives and ambitions of universities, see Bok, *Universities in the Marketplace;* Rhodes, *The Creation of the Future;* and the books cited in note 4 above.

13. Good discussions of these dilemmas can be found in Kennedy, "Making Choices," esp. 134–41, and *Academic Duty,* chap. 10; and in Bok, *Universities in the Marketplace,* esp. 189–94; another in Henry Rosovsky, *The University: An Owner's Manual* (New York: Norton, 1990). Rosovsky writes that economists "are comfortable with the notion of 'trade-offs'; choices involve a little more of this and a little less of that. Humanists often find this kind of reasoning repellent and scientists tend to believe it is immoral when applied to their choices" (26). See also Jonathan R. Cole, "Balancing Acts: Dilemmas of Choice Facing Research Universities," *Daedalus* 122, no. 4 (1993): 5–11; Ehrenberg, *Tuition Rising,* 19–22; and Stanley Fish, *Save the World on Your Own Time* (New York: Oxford University Press, 2008), 109–15, on "shared governance."

14. See Harold T. Shapiro, "The Functions and Resources of the American University of the Twenty-First Century," *Minerva* 30 (1992): 163–74, and "Higher Education in a Changing Environment," paper delivered at a meeting of the COFHE, Boston, October 6, 1988; Rhodes,

The Creation of the Future, 140–45; Kennedy, "Making Choices," 129–30; and the literature listed in note 4 above.

15. The phenomenon of the rich getting richer and of the enlarging gap between the wealthiest universities and the rest, as well as the growing disparities of resources between public and private institutions, is receiving intensified attention today. For a recent discussion, see Cole, *The Great American University*, 472–88.

16. Quoted by Delbanco in "The Endangered University." See also Cole, *The Great American University*, 498.

17. Matthew W. Finkin and Robert C. Post, *For the Common Good: Principles of American Academic Freedom* (New Haven, CT: Yale University Press, 2009), 39, 149. The literature on academic freedom is of course extensive; for recent discussions and debates, and for commentary on the issues of academic freedom especially pertinent to universities at present, I would draw attention especially to Finkin and Post's book cited above, to Donald A. Downs, *Restoring Free Speech and Liberty on Campus* (Cambridge: Cambridge University Press, 2005); Robert O'Neil, *Academic Freedom in the Wired World: Political Extremism, Corporate Power, and the University* (Cambridge, MA: Harvard University Press, 2008); and to the papers in Louis Menand, ed., *The Future of Academic Freedom* (Chicago: University of Chicago Press, 1996), as well as *Free Inquiry at Risk: Universities in Dangerous Times*, special issue, *Social Research* 76, no. 2 (Summer 2009). Fish, *Save the World on Your Own Time*, 72–97, makes lively reading on the subject. Craig Calhoun, "Academic Freedom, Public Knowledge, and the Structural Transformation of the University," in *Free Inquiry at Risk*, 561–97, is of special interest in connecting individual and institutional aspects of academic freedom and relating these to the current state of university life. Schrecker, in *The Lost Soul of American Higher Education*, contends that academic freedom is endangered today by trends in higher education that she sees as moving faculty further and further away from any effective participation in institutional governance.

18. Calhoun, "Academic Freedom," 578–79. See also 585: "[A]cademic freedom is not just a matter of extramural free speech, but also a matter

of the shaping of internal intellectual agendas and the organization of internal communication. The more the university is organized in a proprietary fashion, in order to provide externally specified goods, the less it can be organized in terms of freedom of academic inquiry. This is true even where the state is the funder—if the state behaves like a private proprietor in seeking sharply delimited products."

19. Of the many statements and debates on this subject, to my mind the single best summary is that of the "Kalven Committee: Report on the University's Role in Political and Social Action" (*University of Chicago Record* 1 [November 11, 1967]). The quotation is from p. 2. The report's basic argument is stated as follows:

> The university is the home and sponsor of critics; it is not itself the critic.... To perform its mission in the society, a university must sustain an extraordinary environment of freedom of inquiry and maintain an independence from political fashions, passions, and pressures. A university, if it is to be true to its faith in intellectual inquiry, must embrace, be hospitable to, and encourage the widest diversity of views within its own community. It is a community but only for the limited, albeit great, purposes of teaching and research. It is not a club, it is not a trade association, it is not a lobby. Since the university is a community only for these limited and distinctive purposes, it is a community which cannot take collective action on the issues of the day without endangering the conditions for its existence and effectiveness. (1)

CONCLUSION

1. Clark Kerr in a later addition to *The Uses of the University* (5th ed.; Cambridge, MA: Harvard University Press, 2001), 133, put it succinctly: "The presence of the university carrying out its normal functions changes society fundamentally, but the attempted manipulation of the university, for the sake of specific political reforms, changes the university for the worse more than it changes society for the better." Henry Rosovsky is eloquent on this point in *The University: An Owner's Manual* (New York: Norton, 1990), 297–99. And as Louis Menand writes in "What Are Universities For?" (*Harper's Magazine*, December 1991), 56:

"[The university needs] to renounce the role of model community and arbiter of social disputes that it has assumed, to ignore the impulse to regulate attitudes and expressions that are the epiphenomena of problems far outside the college walls, to stop trying to set up academic housing for every intellectual and political interest group that comes along, and to restrict itself to the business of imparting some knowledge to the people who need it."

SELECT BIBLIOGRAPHY

Anderson, Martin. *Impostors in the Temple: American Intellectuals Are Destroying Our Universities and Cheating Our Students of Their Future.* New York: Simon & Schuster, 1992.

Archibald, Robert B., and David H. Feldman. *Why Does College Cost So Much?* Oxford: Oxford University Press, 2010.

Arum, Richard, and Josipa Roksa. *Academically Adrift: Limited Learning on College Campuses.* Chicago: University of Chicago Press, 2010.

Ashmore, Harry S. *Unseasonable Truths: The Life of Robert Maynard Hutchins.* Boston: Little, Brown, 1989.

Bell, Daniel. *The Reforming of General Education: The Columbia College Experience in Its National Setting.* New York: Columbia University Press, 1966.

Berman, Paul, ed. *Debating P.C.: The Controversy over Political Correctness on College Campuses.* New York: Dell, 1992.

Bloom, Allan. *The Closing of the American Mind: How Higher Education Has Failed Democracy and Impoverished the Souls of Today's Students.* New York: Simon & Schuster, 1987.

Bok, Derek. *Universities in the Marketplace: The Commercialization of Higher Education.* Princeton, NJ: Princeton University Press, 2003.

Bowen, William G., Matthew M. Chingos, and Michael P. McPherson. *Crossing the Finish Line: Completing College at America's Public Universities.* Princeton, NJ: Princeton University Press, 2009.

Bowen, William G., Martin Kurzweil, and Eugene Tobin. *Equity and Excellence in Higher Education.* Charlottesville: University of Virginia Press, 2005.

Bowen, William G., and Harold T. Shapiro, eds. *Universities and Their Leadership.* Princeton, NJ: Princeton University Press, 1998.

Boyer, Ernest L. *Scholarship Reconsidered: Priorities of the Professoriate.* n.p.: Carnegie Foundation for the Advancement of Teaching, 1990.

Boyer, John W. *Academic Freedom and the Modern University: The Experience of the University of Chicago.* Occasional Papers on Higher Education 10. Chicago: College of the University of Chicago, 2002.

———. *"Broad Christian in the Fullest Sense": William Rainey Harper and the University of Chicago.* Occasional Papers on Higher Education 15. Chicago: College of the University of Chicago, 2005.

———. *Judson's War and Hutchins's Peace.* Occasional Papers on Higher Education 12. Chicago: College of the University of Chicago, 2003.

———. *A Twentieth-Century Cosmos: The New Plan and the Origins of General Education at Chicago.* Occasional Papers on Higher Education 16. Chicago: College of the University of Chicago, 2006.

———. *The University of Chicago and War in the Twentieth Century.* Occasional Papers on Higher Education 11. Chicago: College of the University of Chicago, 2003.

Brint, Steven, ed. *The Future of the City of Intellect: The Changing American University.* Stanford, CA: Stanford University Press, 2002.

Calhoun, Craig. "Academic Freedom, Public Knowledge, and the Structural Transformation of the University." *Free Inquiry at Risk: Universities in Dangerous Times.* Special issue. *Social Research* 76, no. 2 (Summer 2009): 561–97.

Carnochan, W. B. *The Battle of the Curriculum: Liberal Education and American Experience.* Stanford, CA: Stanford University Press, 1993.

Chait, Richard. "The '*Academic Revolution*' Revisited." In Brint: 293–321.

Clark, Burton R. *Places of Inquiry: Research and Advanced Education in Modern Universities.* Berkeley: University of California Press, 1995.

————, ed. *The Research Foundations of Graduate Education: Germany, Britain, France, United States, Japan.* Berkeley: University of California Press, 1993.

Clotfelter, Charles T. *Big-Time Sports in American Universities.* Cambridge: Cambridge University Press, 2011.

————. *Buying the Best: Cost Escalation in Elite Higher Education.* Princeton, NJ: Princeton University Press, 1996.

Cole, Jonathan R. "Balancing Acts: Dilemmas of Choice Facing Research Universities." *Daedalus* 122, no. 4 (Fall 1993): 1–36.

————. *The Great American University: Its Rise to Preeminence, Its Indispensable National Role, Why It Must Be Protected.* New York: Public Affairs, 2009.

Delbanco, Andrew. "Colleges: An Endangered Species?" *New York Review of Books* 52 (March 10, 2005).

————. "The Endangered University." *New York Review of Books* 52 (March 24, 2005): 19–22.

————. "The Universities in Trouble." *New York Review of Books* 56, no. 8 (May 14, 2009).

De Ridder-Symoens, H., ed. *A History of the University in Europe.* Vol. 1: *Universities in the Middle Ages.* Cambridge: Cambridge University Press, 1992.

————. *A History of the University in Europe.* Vol. 2: *Universities in Early Modern Europe (1500–1800).* Cambridge: Cambridge University Press, 1996.

Doumani, Beshara, ed. *Academic Freedom after September 11.* New York: Zone Books, 2006.

Downs, Donald A. *Restoring Free Speech and Liberty on Campus.* Cambridge: Cambridge University Press, 2005.

D'Souza, Dinesh. *Illiberal Education: The Politics of Race and Sex on Campus.* New York: Free Press, 1991.

Dzuback, Mary Ann. *Robert M. Hutchins: Portrait of an Educator.* Chicago: University of Chicago Press, 1991.

Ehrenberg, Ronald L. *Tuition Rising.* Cambridge, MA: Harvard University Press, 2002.

———, ed. *Governing Academia.* Ithaca, NY: Cornell University Press, 2004.

Ehrenberg, Ronald L., Harriet Zuckerman, Jeffrey A. Groen, and Sharon M. Brucker. *Educating Scholars: Doctoral Education in the Humanities.* Princeton, NJ: Princeton University Press, 2010.

Engell, James, and Anthony Dangerfield. *Saving Higher Education in the Age of Money.* Charlottesville: University of Virginia Press, 2005.

Finkin, Matthew W., and Robert C. Post. *For the Common Good: Principles of American Academic Freedom.* New Haven, CT: Yale University Press, 2009.

Fish, Stanley. *Save the World on Your Own Time.* New York: Oxford University Press, 2008.

Free Inquiry at Risk: Universities in Dangerous Times. Special issue. *Social Research* 76, no. 2 (Summer 2009).

Geiger, Roger L. *Knowledge and Money: Research Universities and the Paradox of the Marketplace.* Stanford, CA: Stanford University Press, 2004.

———. *Research and Relevant Knowledge: American Research Universities since World War II.* New York: Oxford University Press, 1993.

———. *To Advance Knowledge: The Growth of American Research Universities, 1900–1940.* New York: Oxford University Press, 1986.

General Education in a Free Society: Report of the Harvard Committee. Cambridge, MA: Harvard University Press, 1945.

General Education in the 21st Century: A Report of the University of California Commission on General Education in the 21st Century. Berkeley: Center for Studies in Higher Education, University of California, Berkeley, 2007.

Glimpses of the Harvard Past. Cambridge, MA: Harvard University Press, 1986.

Goodspeed, Thomas Wakefield. *A History of the University of Chicago: The First Quarter Century.* Chicago: University of Chicago Press, 1916.

Graham, Hugh Davis, and Nancy Diamond. *The Rise of American Research Universities: Elites and Challengers in the Postwar Era.* Baltimore, MD: Johns Hopkins University Press, 1997.

Hacker, Andrew, and Claudia Dreifus. *Higher Education? How Colleges Are Wasting Our Money and Failing Our Kids—And What We Can Do about It.* New York: Times Books, 2010.

Harper, William Rainey. "The Quinquennial Statement of the President." *University Record* 1, no. 16 (July 17, 1896): 254.

Haskins, Charles Homer. *The Renaissance of the Twelfth Century.* Cambridge, MA: Harvard University Press, 1927.

Hawkins, Hugh. *Between Harvard and America: The Educational Leadership of Charles W. Eliot.* New York: Oxford University Press, 1972.

Hershberg, James. *James B. Conant: Harvard to Hiroshima and the Making of the Nuclear Age.* New York: Knopf, 1993.

Hofstadter, Richard, and Walter P. Metzger. *The Development of Academic Freedom in the United States.* New York: Columbia University Press, 1955.

Hofstadter, Richard, and Wilson Smith, eds. *American Higher Education: A Documentary History.* Vol. 2. Chicago: University of Chicago Press, 1961.

Hoover, Eric. "Application Inflation: When Is Enough Enough?" *New York Times,* November 5, 2010.

Howe, Irving. "The Value of the Canon." In Berman: 153–71.

Hutchins, Robert Maynard. *Education for Freedom.* Baton Rouge: Louisiana State University Press, 1943.

———. "The Freedom of the University." *Ethics* 61 (1951): 95–104.

———. *The Higher Learning in America.* 2nd ed. New Haven, CT: Yale University Press, 1962.

———. "The Meaning and Significance of Academic Freedom." *Annals of the American Academy of Political and Social Science* 300 (1955): 72–78.

———. *The University of Utopia.* Chicago: University of Chicago Press, 1953.

The Idea and Ideals of the University. Occasional Paper 63. n.p.: American Council of Learned Societies, 2007.

Jencks, Christopher, and David Riesman. *The Academic Revolution.* 2nd ed. Chicago: University of Chicago Press, 1969.

Kalven Committee. "Kalven Committee: Report on the University's Role in Political and Social Action." *University of Chicago Record* 1 (November 11, 1967).

Kennedy, Donald. *Academic Duty.* Cambridge, MA: Harvard University Press, 1997.

———. "Making Choices in the Research University." *Daedalus* 122, no. 4 (Fall 1993): 127–56.

Kernan, Alvin B., ed. *What's Happened to the Humanities?* Princeton, NJ: Princeton University Press, 1997.

Kerr, Clark. *The Gold and the Blue.* 2 vols. Berkeley: University of California Press, 2001, 2004.

———. *The Uses of the University.* 5th ed. Cambridge, MA: Harvard University Press, 2001.

Kimball, Bruce A. *Orators and Philosophers: A History of the Idea of Liberal Education.* New York: Teachers College, Columbia University, 1986.

Kimball, Roger. *Tenured Radicals: How Politics Has Corrupted Our Higher Education.* New York: Harper Perennial, 1990.

Kirp, David L. *Shakespeare, Einstein, and the Bottom Line: The Marketing of Higher Education.* Cambridge, MA: Harvard University Press, 2003.

Kronman, Anthony T. *Education's End: Why Our Colleges and Universities Have Given Up on the Meaning of Life.* New Haven, CT: Yale University Press, 2009.

Kurzweil, Edith, and William Phillips, eds. *Our Country, Our Culture: The Politics of Political Correctness.* Boston, MA: Partisan Review, 1994.

McClelland, Charles. *State, Society and University in Germany: 1700–1914.* Cambridge: Cambridge University Press, 1980.

McNeill, William H. *Hutchins' University.* Chicago: University of Chicago Press, 1991.

Maranto, Robert, Richard E. Redding, and Frederick M. Hess, eds. *The Politically Correct University: Problems, Scope, and Reforms.* Washington, DC: AEI Press, 2009.

Marsden, George M. *The Soul of the American University: From Protestant Establishment to Established Nonbelief.* New York: Oxford University Press, 1994.

Mayer, Milton. *Robert Maynard Hutchins: A Memoir.* Berkeley: University of California Press, 1993.

Menand, Louis. *The Marketplace of Ideas: Reform and Resistance in the American University.* New York: Norton, 2010.

———. *The Marketplace of Ideas.* Occasional Paper 49. n.p.: American Council of Learned Societies, 2001.

———. "What Are Universities For?" *Harper's Magazine,* December 1991, 47–56.

Menand, Louis, ed. *The Future of Academic Freedom.* Chicago: University of Chicago Press, 1996.

More, Thomas. *Selected Letters.* Ed. Elizabeth F. Rogers. New Haven, CT: Yale University Press, 1961.

Morison, Samuel Eliot. *The Founding of Harvard College.* Cambridge, MA: Harvard University Press, 1935.

———. *Three Centuries of Harvard.* Cambridge, MA: Harvard University Press, 1936.

Newman, John Henry. *The Idea of a University.* Ed. Frank M. Turner. New Haven, CT: Yale University Press, 1996.

Nisbet, Robert. *The Degradation of the Academic Dogma.* 2nd ed. New Brunswick, NJ: Transaction Press, 1997.

Nussbaum, Martha. *Not for Profit: Why Democracy Needs the Humanities.* Princeton, NJ: Princeton University Press, 2010.

Oakley, Francis. *Community of Learning: The American College and the Liberal Arts Tradition.* New York: Oxford University Press, 1992.

O'Boyle, Lenore. "Learning for Its Own Sake: The German University as Nineteenth-Century Model." *Comparative Studies in Society and History* 25, no. 1 (January 1983): 3–25.

O'Neil, Robert. *Academic Freedom in the Wired World: Political Extremism, Corporate Power, and the University.* Cambridge, MA: Harvard University Press, 2008.

Pedersen, Olaf. *The First Universities: Studium generale and the Origins of University Education in Europe.* Cambridge: Cambridge University Press, 1997.

Pelikan, Jaroslav. *The Idea of the University: A Reexamination.* New Haven, CT: Yale University Press, 1992.

———. *Scholarship and Its Survival.* n.p.: Carnegie Foundation for the Advancement of Teaching, 1983.

Radder, Hans. *The Commodification of Academic Research.* Pittsburgh, PA: University of Pittsburgh Press, 2010.

Readings, Bill. *The University in Ruins.* Cambridge, MA: Harvard University Press, 1996.

Reuben, Julie A. *The Making of the Modern University: Intellectual Transformation and the Marginalization of Morality.* Chicago: University of Chicago Press, 1996.

Rhodes, Frank H. T. *The Creation of the Future: The Role of the American University.* Ithaca, NY: Cornell University Press, 2001.

Rosovsky, Henry. *The University: An Owner's Manual.* New York: Norton, 1990.

Rothblatt, Sheldon. *The Modern University and Its Discontents: The Fate of Newman's Legacies in Britain and America.* Cambridge: Cambridge University Press, 1997.

Rudolph, Frederick. *The American College and University: A History.* 2nd ed. Athens: University of Georgia Press, 1990.

———. *Curriculum: A History of the American Undergraduate Course of Study since 1636.* San Francisco: Jossey-Bass, 1977.

Schaar, John H., and Sheldon S. Wolin. "Berkeley and the Fate of the Multiversity." *New York Review of Books* 4 (March 11, 1965).

Schrecker, Ellen W. *No Ivory Tower: McCarthyism and the Universities.* New York: Oxford University Press, 1986.

———. *The Lost Soul of American Higher Education: Corporatization, the Assault on Academic Freedom, and the End of the American University.* New York: New Press, 2010.

Schulman, James L., and William G. Bowen. *The Game of Life: College Sports and Educational Values.* Princeton, NJ: Princeton University Press, 2001.

Shapiro, Harold T. "The Functions and Resources of the American University of the Twenty-First Century." *Minerva* 30 (1992): 163–74.

——. "Higher Education in a Changing Environment." Paper delivered at a meeting of the COFHE, Boston, October 6, 1988.

——. *A Larger Sense of Purpose: Higher Education and Society.* Princeton, NJ: Princeton University Press, 2005.

Searle, John R. "Is There a Crisis in American Higher Education?" *Bulletin of the Academy of Arts and Sciences* 46 (January 1993): 24–47.

——. "Rationality and Realism: What Is at Stake?" *Daedalus* 122 (Fall 1993): 55–68.

——. "The Storm over the University." *New York Review of Books* 37, no. 19 (December 6, 1990): 34–42.

Smelser, Neil. "The Politics of Ambivalence: Diversity in the Research Universities." *Daedalus* 46 (Fall 1993): 37–53.

——. *Reflections on the University of California: From the Free Speech Movement to the Global University.* Berkeley: University of California Press, 2010.

Soares, Joseph A. *The Decline of Privilege.* Stanford, CA: Stanford University Press, 1999.

Stone, Geoffrey. *Perilous Times: Free Speech in Wartime from the Sedition Act of 1798 to the War on Terrorism.* New York: Norton, 2004.

Storr, Richard J. *Harper's University: The Beginnings.* Chicago: University of Chicago Press, 1966.

Sykes, Charles J. *Prof Scam: Professors and the Demise of Higher Education.* New York: St. Martin's Press, 1990.

Tappan, Henry P. "University Education." In Hofstadter and Smith: 2:488–51.

Taylor, Mark C. *Crisis on Campus: A Bold Plan for Reforming Our Colleges and Universities.* New York: Knopf, 2010.

Thelin, John R. *A History of American Higher Education.* Baltimore, MD: Johns Hopkins University Press, 2004.

Tuchman, Gayle. *Wannabe U: Inside the Corporate University.* Chicago: University of Chicago Press, 2009.

Turner, Frank M. "Newman's University and Ours." In Newman: 282–301.

The University of the Twenty-First Century: A Symposium to Celebrate the Centenary of the University of Chicago. Special issue. *Minerva* 30 (Summer 1992).

Verger, Jacques. "Patterns." In de Ridder-Symoens: 1:41–45.

Vest, Charles M. *The American Research University from World War II to World Wide Web.* Berkeley: University of California Press, 2007.

Veysey, Laurence R. *The Emergence of the American University.* Chicago: University of Chicago Press, 1965.

Ward, F. Champion, ed. *The Idea and Practice of General Education: An Account of the College of the University of Chicago.* Chicago: University of Chicago Press, 1950.

Washburn, Jennifer. *University, Inc: The Corporate Corruption of American Higher Education.* New York: Basic Books, 2005.

Wegener, Charles. *Liberal Education and the Modern University.* Chicago: University of Chicago Press, 1978.

Weisbrod, Burton A., Jeffrey Ballou, and Evelyn D. Asch. *Mission and Money: Understanding the University.* Cambridge: Cambridge University Press, 2009.

Wilson, Woodrow. "Princeton in the Nation's Service." In *College and State: Educational, Literary, and Political Papers (1875–1913),* vol. 1, ed. Ray Stannard Baker and William E. Dodd, 259–85. New York: Harper, 1925.

Winston, Gordon C. "The Positional Arms Race in Higher Education." Discussion Paper No. 54. Williams Project on the Economics of Higher Education, April 2000.

Zemsky, Robert. *Making Reform Work: The Case for Transforming American Higher Education.* New Brunswick, NJ: Rutgers University Press, 2009.

Text:	10.75/15 Janson
Display:	Janson MT Pro
Compositor:	Toppan Best-set Premedia Limited
Printer/Binder:	Integrated Book Technology